THE BUDDHA'S TEACHINGS ON PROSPERITY

THE BUDDHA'S TEACHINGS ON PROSPERITY

AT HOME, AT WORK, IN THE WORLD

BY BHIKKHU BASNAGODA RAHULA, PH.D.

FOREWORD BY SIR ARTHUR C. CLARKE

 Wisdom Publications • Boston

Wisdom Publications
199 Elm Street
Somerville MA 02144 USA
www.wisdompubs.org

Library of Congress Cataloging-in-Publication Data
Rahula, Basnagoda, Bhikkhu.
 The Buddha's teachings on prosperity : at home, at work, in the world / by
Bhikkhu Basnagoda Rahula ; foreword by Sir Arthur C. Clarke.
   p. cm.
Includes bibliographical references and index.
ISBN 0-86171-547-0 (pbk. : alk. paper)
 1. Religious life—Buddhism. 2. Buddhist laymen—Conduct of life. I. Title.
BQ5400.R35 2008
294.3'444—dc22

                          2008002690

12 11 10 09 08
5 4 3 2 1

Cover design by Gopa&Ted2, Inc.. Interior design by TL. Set in Weiss 12/15.5.

Wise laypeople improve two kinds of skills.
First, they develop the ability to obtain new
wealth and to secure the acquired wealth.
Next, they learn how to differentiate between
wholesome and unwholesome conduct and
how to follow a wholesome way of life.
Lay followers of my teaching secure a tenfold
improvement. [In their external progress],
they [develop skill to] obtain more property,
increase wealth, improve family relationships,
establish a strong workforce, and obtain more
four-footed animals [such as horses and
sheep]. [In their inner growth], my lay followers develop confidence in their spiritual path,
discipline themselves, acquire more knowledge, practice generosity, and gain wisdom.

The Buddha, *The Numerical Discourses*

PUBLISHER'S ACKNOWLEDGMENT

The publisher gratefully acknowledges the generous help of the Hershey Family Foundation in sponsoring the production of this book.

TABLE OF CONTENTS

FOREWORD

BY ARTHUR C. CLARKE

I have to admit that there is some incongruity in a lifelong secularist like myself writing these words to introduce a book on the Buddha's way to prosperity, wisdom, and inner peace. My views on religion have been widely publicized, and I believe all religions are a form of mind virus that affects otherwise healthy—and often educated—human beings.

Buddhism stands apart in being tolerant, accommodating, and pragmatic. Having lived for a half-century in Sri Lanka, I have seen how the Buddha's teachings are applied by various groups in many different ways. Strange as it might seem, perfectly rational people and rabid fundamentalists both claim to derive their beliefs and attitudes from the same source. Clearly, many liberties are being taken with the original teachings.

That is why I welcome the publication of this book, by Bhikkhu Basnagoda Rahula, Ph.D., which aims to rediscover the principles and values of Buddhism that have been obscured by centuries of culture and history.

Many years ago, I had the pleasure of associating with the late Dr. Walpola Rahula, one of the few truly erudite people I have met. He struggled long and hard to rid Buddhism of fanaticism and rituals. I hope the current Bhikkhu Rahula will continue that noble mission, as there is much unfinished business.

—King's College, London

Determined to bring benefit and happiness to a great number of people, the Buddha established a well-organized society. This social movement attracted hundreds of thousands of men and women who belonged to all social classes.

The Buddha's new society consisted of two groups, ordained disciples and lay followers, both of which he considered equally important. While the Buddha made every effort to lead his ordained disciples to the highest spiritual progress, he also made every effort to guide his lay followers toward prosperity, wisdom, and inner peace—yet history seems to have largely buried this part of his guidance!

The passage of twenty-six centuries has obscured the Buddha's teachings for the lay community—and often what reference can be found makes these teachings seem insignificant or presents them in a way that can be misleading. This book intends to restore them to prominence, with context and clarity. Breaking through historical and cultural barriers, it traces what the Buddha actually taught for the benefit of his lay followers, and regroups and elucidates his teachings on lay life.

Numerous requests from various quarters, especially from the audiences of my public talks, sowed the seeds of this book on the Buddha's philosophy and guidance of lay life. Considering the scarcity of similar works and the usefulness of such a book to society, I ventured to undertake the task. This book is the result.

CHAPTER ORGANIZATION

Chapter 1 examines the causes behind the obscurity and mis-interpretation of the Buddha's guidance for the layperson's life. Why have these teachings on everyday life drawn so little attention? Why had they remained hidden for so long? Chapter 1 answers these questions.

Chapter 2 focuses on the freedom the Buddha offered to the layperson to be prosperous, and denies the popular but erroneous view that the Buddha discouraged striving for success. Based on this false view, some people mistakenly believe that being wealthy goes against the Buddha's teachings—a misunderstanding that may make the Buddha's teachings seem irrelevant to lay life. Chapter 2 examines this in detail.

The following chapters identify the requirements for a successful life. In them, the Buddha clarifies virtually everything that makes a layperson's life prosperous, meaningful, and peaceful.

Chapter 3 introduces his instructions, techniques, and tips for reaching material success, and clarifies how to initiate that journey.

Chapters 4 through 13 discuss the various topics that the Buddha identified as important for a layperson's success, including personal and social relationships, decision-making, and personality development.

The final chapter brings the discussion to the most important topic: the achievement of inner peace and lasting happiness. This, the Buddha emphasized, should be life's ultimate goal. To reach this elusive but feasible goal, he introduced effective techniques. For readers who might feel confused about how to obtain inner peace and happiness, these techniques should be revealing.

The purpose of this book is to present practical, helpful instructions for daily life. The contents have been selected, organized, and designed to serve this purpose. Metaphysical concepts have been omitted since they represent an altogether different field. Anyone looking for practical guidance to prosperity and *lasting* happiness should find this book extremely beneficial.

TRANSLATION OF PALI TEXTS

Almost every translation of the Pali texts used in this work is original. While new reliable translations, such as those of Bhikkhu Bodhi, are now being published, some existent translations fail to present the correct meanings of important Pali words and phrases. Some also lack clarity and simplicity. Word-for-word translations of Pali passages may not convey their original meaning nor preserve their original tone. These difficulties prompted me to spend hours with Pali scholars in an effort to present the best possible meaning of the Pali quotations used in this book.

Several characteristics of these translations are worth mentioning. One is the avoidance of repetition. In the original Pali texts, some sentences and phrases are redundant, making a word-for-word translation of these passages meaningless. I have omitted such repetitions in order to convey the clearest meaning without being wordy.

Further, most quotations in this book give the best possible meanings, rather than direct translations, of the Pali passages. For instance, one English rendition in chapter 1 reads: "Master, we are the laypeople who live with a family..." The Pali phrase I have translated as "live with a family" is *puttadara samba-dhasayanam ajjhavasama*, which literally means "to sleep together in a bed where children and wife cause disturbances." What the speaker actually wants to convey, of course, is that he has a family to whom he must fulfill his duties. Thus, instead of a literal translation, I have provided the most relevant equivalent of the Pali phrase. I have followed this method of translating throughout the book.

The translations are also in keeping with modern linguistic norms, particularly with regard to gender impartiality, clarity, and simplicity. Pronouns referenced as "he or she" and "his or her" are meant to avoid gender bias. To avoid repetition of these pronoun references, some singular nouns in original quotations have been changed to the plural. Also, some long, complex Pali sentences have been divided into two or more short, simple sentences without changing their meaning.

The sources of translations are given in the endnotes. Even if a quotation occurs in several Pali *suttas*, only one source is cited. Special notes appear within the endnotes whenever the translation requires an explanation.

CITATION OF PALI SOURCES

Because the English translations given in this book are original, I have cited the place, number, and name of original Pali sources (e.g.: *Anguttara Nikaya VIII:* Gotami Vagga: Gotami Sutta). For those who wish to refer to other English translations, I have selected the texts translated by Bhikkhu Bodhi and published by Wisdom Publications. Both references appear under the same number in the endnote section. When citing texts not yet translated by Bhikkhu Bodhi, I have given only the original Pali sources. When the name does not appear in the original Pali texts, only the original numerical order has been cited. This method of citation may help an interested reader to find the original sources.

This book does not use diacritical symbols to aid with the pronunciation of Pali words. Since the objective of using Pali quotations and original Pali texts is to authenticate and clarify the points of discussion, a pronunciation guide to Pali words does not seem necessary.

CHAPTER 1: A TREASURE BURIED IN TIME

The moon, the sun, and my teaching...
They all shine brightly when they are uncovered.
The Buddha, *The Numerical Discourses*

For some readers, the Buddha's guidance to the skillful living of lay life might seem an altogether new and unusual topic. Many embrace the common assumption that the Buddha taught only about impermanence, suffering, and the denial of pleasure. Influenced by this belief, you may assume that he ignored the happiness of lay life and discouraged people from seeking success. What's more, you may make the common assumption that the Buddha advised all his listeners to renounce the pleasures of daily life and seek happiness in the spiritual life.

However, an in-depth study of the Buddha's teachings reveals this interpretation to be inaccurate. The Buddha clearly recognized and admired happiness in life. He not only encouraged people to obtain wealth but instructed them on how to save, invest, and manage their wealth as well. He also offered guidance to his lay community on successful interpersonal and social relationships, decision-making, and healthy personality development. Above all, he showed the lay community the path to happiness.

Contrary to what some believe today, the Buddha's teachings include invaluable instructions for success and happiness in everyday life.

UNIQUE SOCIETY, UNIQUE RELIGION

A curious reader might wonder why the Buddha would focus on secular life. We might expect a religion to have a system of beliefs beyond sensory experience, rather than a system of guidance for worldly life. The Buddha's teachings, however, offer an approach to religion notably different from most others'.

Both his basic philosophy and the unique social factors present in India in the sixth century B.C.E. paved the way for the Buddha not only to guide his listeners' spiritual progress but also to oversee their daily lives. The Buddha never presented himself or his disciples as messengers or representatives of a divine power. Therefore, the importance and value of his teaching to society had to be specifically and empirically demonstrated mainly in terms of its social usefulness.

Whereas a Brahmin teacher might recommend and direct a huge offering to a deity to avert an impending catastrophe, the Buddha refused to stress such beliefs and practices. Instead, he emphasized human effort and human responsibility as the key to dealing with difficult situations. Whenever a listener raised a question about his or her personal life, the Buddha would analyze the problem and offer a solution based on human responsibility and skill. Because he and his ordained disciples constantly offered such rational solutions to their lay followers, "worldly life" became a popular topic in the Buddha's teaching.

Social expectations further encouraged this focus on daily life. The Buddha lived in an age during which hundreds of thinkers and religious leaders were competing for followers. Some of those campaigners argued openly against spiritualism and convinced people that such concepts as enlightenment, after-death existence, and rebirth were myths. As a result, that society became so atheistic and secular that most people found their present lives more attractive than what seemed to await them—and they were more attentive to those teachers who provided assistance for their everyday life than to those who talked about life after death.

The Buddha's audiences brought these expectations to the Buddha and inquired whether he had anything to offer toward their worldly success. The Buddha's teaching ideally suited such a society. He relentlessly applied his philosophy toward the benefit of his lay community, which added depth to the topic of worldly life. Thus the prosperity of the Buddha's society resulted in secular life becoming a broad and profound subject in his teaching.

The sixth century B.C.E. was an age of renaissance in India. Business people carried on extensive trading with Persia and the Greek world by land and by sea. With business booming and wealth increasing, affluent communities expanded in Magadha and Kosala—the two states in which the Buddha traveled widely. Consequently, business management and wise decision-making—along with family life and managing social relationships—emerged as important aspects of daily life. The Buddha, with his power, popularity, and rational approach to such topics, distinguished himself in that society as the most qualified adviser to the lay community.

Moreover, the Buddha had to play an especially active role in nurturing the prosperous lay community, because his ordained community could not have existed without affluent lay supporters. Neither the Buddha nor his ordained disciples were ascetics who practiced self-torture; they were social campaigners who lived a moderate life, avoiding both self-denial and self-indulgence. For the welfare of his ordained disciples, the Buddha freely accepted lands and houses donated by wealthy admirers; and he regularly accepted invitations to their palaces and mansions for meals, often with hundreds of bhikkhus. With the existence of his ordained community resting upon the prosperity of lay supporters, it was essential for the Buddha to skillfully guide their material success.

The Buddha's approach to various aspects of secular life seems to have been inspired by his own relationships with the wealthy. Some of the Buddha's most faithful followers and supporters were kings, princes, and business people who strove to increase their wealth and satisfy their senses. King Kosala, for instance, often asked the Buddha such questions as "Which sense should be satisfied most?"[1] Many others inquired about making their lives happier. Given this unique social background, "success and happiness in secular life" became an important topic in his teaching. The Buddha also voluntarily helped families in various ways in their daily lives, and he persuaded his ordained disciples to do the same.

TWO ATTITUDES TOWARD HAPPINESS

The Buddha viewed the subject of happiness realistically: as something that actually exists. Addressing his ordained disciples to encourage their search for happiness in the renounced life, he taught:

> Two kinds of happiness exist: one in lay life [gihi sukha] and the other in renounced life [pabbajja sukha]. Of these two, happiness in renounced life is better.

> Two kinds of happiness exist: one derived from sensory satisfaction [kama sukha] and the other derived from giving up sensory satisfaction [nekkhamma sukha]. Of these two, the happiness derived from giving up sensory satisfaction is better.[2]

These two statements offer a vital clue to the Buddha's attitude toward happiness. He explicitly noted that happiness exists in lay life, and in the satisfaction of the senses. Even in the presence of bhikkhus, who needed strong emphasis on the dissatisfactions of secular life, the Buddha never denied the fact of happiness in the material and sensory worlds. He merely placed happiness in the renounced life above it.

More evidence found elsewhere in the *Sutta Pitaka* confirms this attitude. Defining happiness, the Buddha again said:

> Happiness exists in worldly life....What is that happiness?
> It is the satisfaction gained through the five senses (*kamaguna*). Sensory objects related to sight, sound, smell, taste, and physical contact do exist. These objects are attractive, desirable, pleasant, appealing, and worthy. Experiences through the five senses means the fivefold advantage one can obtain in lay life. The happiness one derives from experiencing these five kinds of benefits is called happiness in worldly life.[3]

The Buddha's view of happiness in secular life is clear and complete. A layperson constantly experiences sensory pleasures, or *kamaguna*, and their five benefits: beautiful sights, pleasing sounds, pleasant scents, delicious tastes, and agreeable physical contact. These benefits are inherent in worldly life, and people are entitled to enjoy them.

APPRECIATING THE BENEFITS OF LAY LIFE

Not only did the Buddha acknowledge the existence of happiness in secular life, he also admired it. Although he stressed (especially in the presence of bhikkhus) that the happiness of lay life is secondary to the happiness of the renounced life, this assertion was not meant to devalue lay life. It simply meant that a more profound happiness awaits those who are willing to give up worldly pleasures.

Because renunciation grants a more stable form of happiness, this "happiness in detachment," or *vimutti sukha*, is said to be "better." This is the happiness experienced by the Buddha himself and by his ordained disciples. With fewer duties, those who renounce worldly life find fewer hindrances to inner peace. Happiness in lay life, on the other hand, fluctuates constantly because of the numerous conflicts and burdens inherent in that life. But other than this single comparison, which does indeed raise spiritual happiness above worldly happiness, no evidence suggests that the Buddha found fault with secular life or the happiness associated with it.

Because the Buddha appreciated lay life, he readily advised and instructed those wanting to know how to make their lives happier and more prosperous. Many people visited the Buddha and requested his guidance toward success and happiness. The following request occurs in many suttas and expresses what the lay community expected from him:

> Master, we are the laypeople who live with a family, wear beautiful clothes, use perfumes and ornaments, and accept gold and silver. Please advise us in such a way that we may make our present existence and the next life happy.[4]

In reply to these requests, the Buddha never showed the slightest disrespect for the speakers' lifestyle and often gave detailed explanations on how to make their lives more successful. He identified these instructions as *sampada*, the factors that bring benefits for secular life. Forty-five years of his vigorous social involvement left invaluable instructions in the *Sutta Pitaka*—and these are what we will explore in this book.

ADDRESSING DIVERSE AUDIENCES

Despite the Buddha's considerable attention to the layperson's happiness and material success, the *Sutta Pitaka* admittedly also contains passages with seemingly conflicting views. Some of the Buddha's speeches advocate a sense of dissatisfaction with the material world and mental detachment from worldly pleasure. While this contradictory view occurs repeatedly in numerous suttas, we must look at these discourses from social and historical points of view to discover their intended audiences and purposes.

Misinterpretation of the Buddha's teachings has arisen, in particular, from confusion about his various audiences.

As noted above, the Buddha spent considerable time countering the concepts presented by various traditionalist and extremist groups, and for this purpose he needed a committed and accomplished community. The Vedic system had its Brahmins, the educated ascetics who defiantly defended its tradition. The Jain order trained its own male and female ascetics to organize its social system. Influenced by both these traditions, the Buddha molded the concept of *Sangha*. This ordained community fulfilled an important need: the organization of a highly dedicated and qualified community to take the Buddha's message to society. The concepts of impermanence, dissatisfaction with worldly pleasure, and detachment from secular life served predominantly to train and maintain this community.

This does not suggest that *nibbana*, the blissful state one can achieve by eliminating mental attachment to worldly pleasure, is merely a technique to train the Sangha. We can hardly disregard the repeated assertions of the Buddha and his disciples that their nonattached existence was extremely happy—a happiness that one may experience irrespective of time and place, upon detaching oneself from the greedy pursuit of sensory pleasures.

Nevertheless, being nonattached to worldly pleasure did serve as an effective technique to train, organize, and strengthen the community of monks and nuns, the very foundation of the Buddha's position in society. And while the repeated emphasis on the mental suffering in the material world was meant for that community and anyone interested in entering it, the same teaching was not appropriate in the same way to the Buddha's lay community.

Mental detachment from sensual pleasure provided a dependable cause for the ordained community to live a renounced life. And while a modern priest might prefer a spiritual life simply to better serve a divine power, no such religious motive was present in the Buddha's teaching. The Buddha encouraged men and women to enter the Sangha because he knew that a renounced life would allow for more inner peace than a lay life would do. He, therefore, encouraged his disciples to meditate constantly on the impermanence and dissatisfaction of worldly pleasure. This attitudinal change toward secular life made his ordained disciples self-controlled and dedicated monks and nuns, who successfully promoted the social influence intended by the Buddha.

Not everything in the *Sutta Pitaka* is for everybody. To avoid misleading claims, we need to identify the various audiences for the various discourses. Just because the Buddha repeatedly told his ordained disciples to meditate on impermanence and dissatisfaction, we cannot conclude that he wanted everybody to follow that teaching.

In fact, there is no evidence in the *Nikayas*, the most authenticated collections of the Buddha's teachings, that he appealed to his lay followers to meditate on impermanence or dissatisfaction.

The Buddha did, of course, recommend useful meditation methods to his lay community, but these were never meant to obstruct the happiness of lay life. Instead, original texts show that his lay disciples were persuaded to live their lives joyfully and meaningfully.

To consider the audience and the purpose of the suttas, we may roughly categorize them into three divisions:

1. Instructive discourses for ordained and soon-to-be-ordained disciples
2. Rational and argumentative speeches to counter opposing views
3. Instructive and rational discourses for the lay community

Of these three groups, the suttas that address the ordained community of males (bhikkhus) clearly outnumber the others. This may lead to the erroneous conclusion that the Buddha's only endeavor was to train his bhikkhus rather than to help his lay followers. There seem to be, however, other reasons for this than the Buddha's overwhelming attention to bhikkhus alone.

WHY LAY LIFE *SEEMS* LESS IMPORTANT

Why does the Buddha's guidance of the layperson never seem to occupy its due position in the *Sutta Pitaka?* To provide a clear answer to this question, we must step into history. The important thing is to consider who, for nearly twenty-six centuries, preserved the Buddha's speeches—and how.

First, the Buddha's speeches were preserved by the bhikkhus. And yet, even though the Buddha traveled continuously for forty-five years and talked to great multitudes of people, only a very small percentage of these teachings and conversations seems to have been recorded. Over 80 percent of all suttas in the *Sutta Pitaka* are addressed to bhikkhus living inside a monastery. Seemingly, the bhikkhus were more interested in preserving what they found useful for themselves and not what the Buddha taught the public.

From the bhikkhus' point of view, such partial preservation of the teachings is understandable. Immediately after the Buddha's death, senior bhikkhus found that their most urgent need was to retain unity and discipline among themselves. With their community expanding, different views and practices were emerging from within and demanded action. The first major council, held just three months after the Buddha passed away, was prompted in part by the unruly behavior of some bhikkhus. In this situation, repeated emphasis on the Buddha's advice to bhikkhus was urgent. And the ordained disciples who memorized Pali suttas for preservation seem to have added, modified, and dropped many suttas in order to stress the disciplines for their own community.

This approach, however, altered the overall appearance of the Buddha's teaching. In the preserved *Sutta Pitaka*, instructions for bhikkhus seem more prominent, and the guidance of the lay community more obscure. A reader might consequently assume, mistakenly, that the Buddha ignored his lay disciples.

The method of grouping the suttas also made the Buddha's speeches for the lay community appear less important. At the first Sangha council, many suttas were categorized according to length. The Buddha's long dialogues were grouped in the *Digha Nikaya*, literally "the section of long discourses." Hundreds of shorter suttas were placed in the *Majjhima Nikaya*, the section for middle-length sayings. Thousands of other suttas were arranged according to a numerical order in the *Anguttara Nikaya*. For example, any discourses that explained *two* causes, *two* effects, *two* kinds of individuals, and so on were grouped under

"Number Two." Sub-numerical headings were also added to further organize the division.

This categorization of the discourses was clearly based on their external appearance, not on their content. As a result, the Buddha's speeches to the lay community are found thinly scattered throughout the *Sutta Pitaka*.

Moreover, most suttas related to lay life were separated from similar suttas and placed among hundreds of suttas intended for the ordained disciples. This arrangement, again, makes the advice for lay life seem insignificant and contradictory. And to the modern reader, the recurring concept of dissatisfaction may still seem to be the Buddha's universal philosophy for all people.

MODERN MISINTERPRETATIONS

Some writers and translators in recent history have become caught in this confusion, thinking mistakenly that the path the Buddha recommended for ordained disciples was his teaching for everyone. In the aftermath of that misunderstanding, such concepts as "Buddhist pessimism" emerged.

Arthur Schopenhauer, the renowned German thinker, reportedly formed his theory of pessimism after reading the few Buddhist texts available to him in translation. Expressing his appreciation of the Buddha, he paved the way for critics to compare his philosophy to the Buddha's. As a result, "Buddhist pessimism" earned recognition in the Western world alongside Schopenhauer's theory of pessimism.

Further, almost every translator of suttas rendered the recurrent keyword *dukkha* as "suffering," and had readers believing that the Buddha regarded worldly life as miserable. However, *dukkha* indicates the insatiable nature of the human mind, not merely so-called suffering. The Buddha employed this word for the purpose of directing the bhikkhus toward nibbana—and not for the instruction of his lay disciples.

Worst of all, hundreds of books written about the Buddha's teachings identify his instructions for the ordained community as the central teaching for the *entire* Buddhist community. This misconception has led to the common assumption that the Buddha discounted worldly life and scorned its happiness.

UNCOVERING THE TRUTH

Closer attention to the *Sutta Pitaka* would make it clear that the Buddha's teaching for the layperson is more secular than most people expect it to be. We find in the *Sutta Pitaka* more than one hundred discourses, ranging from long dialogues to short utterances, dealing exclusively with lay life. The following chapters will focus on these suttas in order to clarify the Buddha's attitude toward worldly life and to elucidate his guidance of the layperson toward success and happiness.

CHAPTER 2: THE BUDDHA'S VIEW ON PROSPERITY

> Poverty is a cause of pain for laypeople.
> Being poor, they run into debt.
> This situation would lead them into a decline.
> The Buddha, *The Numerical Discourses*

The Buddha's view of prosperity stands out as one of the most misinterpreted aspects of his teachings. Many writers have either stated or implied that the Buddha did not encourage people to prosper and become wealthy. This misinterpretation influenced some to believe that achieving prosperity goes against the Buddha's teachings. But let us examine what the Buddha actually maintained with regard to the layperson's wealth and prosperity.

THE FREEDOM TO PROSPER

First, the Buddha never imposed limitations on his lay followers' efforts to be successful; instead, he clearly encouraged them to strive for success. Whether in "trading, cattle farming, archery, government service, or any other profession or industry," the layperson should strive to advance in his or her respective field.[1] Notably, the motivation to achieve success is an important requirement in any person's life—and an attitude of

"I have a job that's enough for me to live on" has no place in the Buddha's teaching.

Next, the Buddha set no limits to a layperson's wealth and never told his prosperous lay followers to stop or slow down. Instead, he unequivocally encouraged them to plan, organize, and even endeavor to obtain more. We will discuss these instructions in detail in later chapters.

The emphasis, here, is on the fact that the Buddha enforced no restrictions on the layperson's personal wealth. Using the phrase "immense wealth" (ulare bhoge),[2] he indicated the amount one could strive to amass—in other words, as much wealth as possible.

PROSPERITY AND PURPOSE

It is important to note that the freedom the Buddha offered to become as prosperous as possible hinges on two conditions. First, one must follow certain guidelines in endeavoring to become prosperous. Second, one must use wealth properly. Unless these two conditions are met, one's "immense wealth" would never gain the Buddha's praise—thus the "boundless freedom" to become wealthy relates to the quantity of wealth, not to the means used to accumulate it. On the other hand, prosperity should never be an end in itself, but merely a means to some wholesome purpose.

Indicating both the individual freedom to be prosperous and the importance of using that freedom correctly, the Buddha said:

> What is atthi sukha [the happiness of possessing wealth]?
>
> A certain person accumulates great wealth and property through fair means and right effort and thinks, "Now I have wealth; now I have property gathered through fair means."

In thinking so, that person experiences happiness
and satisfaction. This is what I call atthi sukha.[3]

Individual prosperity is clearly supported, as long as the
layperson employs "fair means and right effort." To understand
what the Buddha means by "fair means and right effort," let's first
look at some of his contemporaries' views on gathering wealth.

Some teachers argued that respect for ethical values were
unimportant. They advised people, including the mighty king
Ajatasattu, to gather wealth using whatever means necessary
and not to worry about the harm these means might cause others.[4] Kassapa, a famous teacher during the Buddha's time, found
no fault with stealing and housebreaking.[5] Other materialists
such as Ajita and Kaccayana held similar views, blatantly dis-
regarding any ethics in becoming prosperous. The Carvaka tradition, a famous Indian materialistic school of thought during
the sixth century B.C.E., summed it up like this: The easiest way
to achieve wealth is to "borrow throughout life and enjoy with
no intention to pay back."

In the light of these materialistic views, we can more usefully
evaluate the Buddha's honorable path to prosperity.

COLLECTING HONEY WITHOUT HARMING THE FLOWERS
The Buddha introduced a system of ethics into the process of
acquiring wealth. Certainly his general ethics—which always
advocate compassion for others—apply to any endeavor, but
the Buddha also set specific guidelines regarding business.

First, the person engaged in profit-making should not deceive
or harm customers or any others involved. He or she must
"gradually increase wealth without squeezing others, just as
bees collect honey without harming flowers."[6] Thus, whatever
wealth one possesses should be acquired "through just means."[7]
Fairness is so vital to making a profit that, before beginning an

ambitious profession or business, one should first make a resolution not to exploit others.

The Buddha's recommendations for the welfare of employees
further clarify an honorable path to prosperity. Specifically, he
mentioned five ways in which employers should treat workers:

Assign work and duties in accordance with their skills
    and abilities
Pay salaries befitting their work and service
Provide medical assistance
Make wholesome food available
Allow for leave and vacations at appropriate times.[8]

These amazingly modern concepts confirm the Buddha's
teaching that people are not entitled to wealth if they fail to follow ethical business practices. In any profit-making endeavor,
employers should refrain from forcing hard labor on others.
They should pay suitable salaries to their employees, and provide them with medical care, food, and leave. From the
Buddha's viewpoint, those who fail to provide welfare for their
workers are unqualified to be wealthy.

Overall, ambitious people are reminded to be mindful of
their ethics. Leaders in business must satisfy their customers
and protect the rights and privileges of their employees. If they
follow these steps, they are at least partially qualified to become
more prosperous. The other qualification for prosperity is the
proper use of wealth.

WEALTH LIKE A RAINFALL THAT NOURISHES LIFE

The proper use of wealth can also be clarified in the light of
what some of the Buddha's contemporaries taught. According
to some, one's own sensory satisfaction is the most important
purpose of having wealth, and one should use every possible

means to achieve this as long as one lives. In this context, charity makes no sense at all.

The Buddha held a different view. He emphasized that the
wealth one acquires through just means should be used to benefit others, as well as oneself:

> The layperson who acquires immense wealth with
> effort, skill, hard work, and respect for justice uses [that
> wealth] to satisfy his or her own senses and to please
> himself or herself. Using wealth, he or she experiences
> happiness in life. At the same time, that person makes
> his or her parents, family [husband or wife and chil-
> dren], and employees happy and satisfied.
>
> Second, the wealthy person uses his or her wealth
> to treat friends and associates. Again, the wealthy per-
> son uses his or her wealth to please relatives and the
> needy [atithi], to honor dead relatives, to fulfill duties
> to the government, and to conduct rituals.
>
> Finally, the wealthy person uses his or her wealth
> to feed those bhikkhus and Brahmins who have dedi-
> cated their lives to self-purification and realization of
> enlightenment.[9]

The Buddha repeatedly emphasized that one's effort should
be meaningful to oneself, to those one lives with, and, broadly
speaking, to the whole of society. "Proper use of wealth" exemplifies this central teaching of the Buddha.

Those who failed to use their wealth in this balanced way
fell short of the Buddha's admiration. King Kosala told the
Buddha that he (the king) had just taken over the huge wealth
of a merchant who died without an heir. The merchant's gold
alone was immensely valuable; but he, himself, had always
worn rags, eaten cheap rice, traveled in a small shabby caravan,

wealth for others' welfare. In response, the
one who fails to use wealth to benefit oneself
to live a meaningful life.[10]

, those who used their wealth to benefit them-
others won the Buddha's great appreciation. Like "a
rain, at nourishes life," great individual wealth should foster a host of people.[11]

Proper use of wealth is essentially the purpose of having wealth. As long as one follows this guideline, the Buddha indicated that one is entitled to make every effort to earn more wealth.

The *Sutta Pitaka* provides no evidence for the percentage of wealth to be allocated for one's own use, for the use of one's children, and for the use of others. However, the Buddha did suggest dividing one's income into four equal portions: two portions to be invested, one to be saved, and the remaining portion for living expenses.[12] The Buddha did not want people to let their holdings dwindle away through mere spending and giving. He regarded savings as essential because "savings can be used in the event of an unexpected tragedy or misfortune."[13]

Only one of the four equal portions of one's income is recommended for expenditures, such as personal expenses and donations. In other words, the Buddha recommended making oneself and others happy with only a certain portion of one's wealth, and not with everything one earns.

The quotation above also recognizes that taking care of children, protecting the rights of employees, and paying a portion of personal income to the government are essential components of the proper use of wealth. Those who do not follow these practices do not deserve to be more prosperous. Thus the fulfillment of one's duties toward society is an important practice for the layperson, and allocating a portion of one's assets for society demonstrates that practice.

An important verse in the *Parabhava Sutta* sheds more light on the Buddha's emphasis that one's own wealth is not merely for oneself. Citing the signs of a layperson's degeneration, he said: "If one who possesses wealth, much gold, and food uses them for oneself [i.e., oneself alone], one is on the way to downfall."[14]

This statement confirms the Buddha's disapproval of a wealthy person's disregard for society. Using wealth "for oneself" may mean one's own personal use or the use of one's family members. Since the wealthy are certainly indebted to society for their prosperity, they are obliged to contribute to society instead of using their wealth only for themselves.

Another question needing clarification is how and to what extent one may satisfy one's senses with the wealth garnered through just means. Some may assume that wealth earned through fair means entitles them to satisfy their senses freely. But this conclusion clearly contradicts the Buddha's teaching about personal use of wealth.

The Buddha never promoted a *carpe diem* theory of sensory satisfaction as the purpose of having wealth. He admired, instead, the person who "acquires immense wealth but is not intoxicated by it,"[15] remarking that those who exceed the limits of sensory satisfaction would "suffer later from the related adverse effects."[16] To be aware of the right measure of sensory gratification is to be aware of the measure that ultimately leads to physical well-being and long life. The Buddha's advice to King Kosala about overeating confirms this:

King Kosala was an ardent pleasure-seeker, particularly where food and drink were concerned. Well known for his huge belly and easygoing personality, he developed a close friendship with the Buddha. Once after a huge meal, panting and visibly discomforted, he visited the Buddha. Observing the king's situation, the Buddha spoke a verse that praised eating in right measure, and he stated that one who knew the right measure of food would get rid of physical discomfort and enjoy a long, healthy life.[17] These words apply, of course, to the enjoyment of any sensual pleasure. The key phrase here is "right measure": right measure is what keeps one within the zone of physical comfort and health, mental well-being, and social acceptance.

SUMMARY

The Buddha elaborated on how people should feel about their wealth and guided them toward gaining the proper advantages from their wealth. He stressed that wealth is a clear source of happiness for laypersons. To achieve that happiness, however, they must earn wealth the right way and use it in the most effective way. Money or wealth is neither to keep nor to use solely for one's own sensory satisfaction; it is to make oneself and others happy and satisfied. While using wealth for oneself, one should be aware of the right measure of sensory satisfaction. Prosperity, according to the Buddha, is the reward when following these recommended guidelines.

CHAPTER 3: GAINING WEALTH

I found out two important principles: not to be content with what I had achieved and not to give up the effort for the highest achievement. Right effort is the first step toward success. Right effort brings benefits and happiness to a layperson.

The Buddha, *The Numerical Discourses*

Praising prosperity as an accomplishment for the layperson, the Buddha strove to guide his lay followers toward material success. In this undertaking, he discussed a wide range of topics required for the initiation and continuation of any ambitious effort. His guidance of the layperson's material success is a complete and thoroughly effective process. We open this discussion in this chapter, which focuses on his instructions for launching a successful effort.

INNER PREPARATION

According to the Buddha's observation, inner preparation represents one of the most important prerequisites for any kind of success. Thus he recommended the same preparation for a layperson's journey toward prosperity—indicating, overall, that psychological preparation is crucial for material success.

First, he advocated the removal of any psychological barriers that might obstruct one's progress. Next, he clarified how right attitude injects power into one's endeavor. These two steps are the basic requirements for inner preparation.

1. REMOVE INNER BARRIERS

Self-imposed limitations, as the Buddha interpreted them, are the biggest hindrance to individual progress in spiritual *or* secular life. Such limitations signify the devaluation of one's own capabilities, skills, and potential. The breeding ground of this low mentality, according to the Buddha, is society.

Social doctrines that blatantly undermine human potential can invade the mind and eventually overpower it. The Buddha advised his lay followers to ignore such views and to rely on their own potential in order to eliminate these barriers. To better understand this message, we need only to look, again, at some views present in the Buddha's society, views that devalued individual ability and prevented progress in material life.

For example, a person born into the Shudra caste should, according to social custom, never make any effort to do business. A Shudra's predestined occupation was believed to be the performance of servile duties for people of higher castes. Similarly, only Brahmins were permitted to become spiritual leaders. Not even members of the ruling caste could do so because Brahma, the creator, had allegedly assigned that task to the Brahmin caste.

The Buddha vehemently opposed the views of his contemporaries who advocated the predetermination of happiness or suffering. He argued that intention and right effort should serve as the essential foundation for material success.

Altogether, he explored, analyzed, and rationally refuted three such views: the will of Brahma, the Vedic theory of karma, and the universal law of predetermination:[1]

The will of Brahma. Those who attributed human progress or downfall to the will of Brahma maintained that higher social positions and various professions were decided by Brahma on the basis of caste. Therefore, they alleged, society should desist from making any changes to social law.

The Vedic theory of karma. Advocates of the karma theory asserted that one's happiness and sorrow were solely determined by one's actions in past lives. This teaching also denies human effort.

The universal law of predetermination. The third theory asserted that whatever is destined to happen will happen, despite any effort to change it. This theory was based on the determinist view that every individual— saint or villain—would exist for a definite number of births before total cessation.

From the Buddha's standpoint, all three views are extremist theories, which invalidate human will and effort to succeed.[2] His argument was strong and rational. He claimed that theorists who held such views could not expect any spiritual progress for themselves—after all, how could meditation and other preferred methods purify them, if effort had no value within these teachings? Thus he said to them, "You have denied human need and human effort to change."[3]

The Buddha's denial of extremist views had one specific aim: removal of the inner barriers that hampered his followers' progress in spiritual and material success. His message to his lay disciples was to shatter the inner cages that imprisoned their potential—and by doing so, to prepare themselves for a promising future.

2. HAVE FAITH IN YOUR OWN POTENTIAL

After eliminating inner obstructions, the Buddha guided his lay followers toward self-reliance. This is the next step in laying the foundation for a successful future. In an era in which individual strength was clearly denied, the Buddha saw that no other factor than self-reliance could prepare an individual for success.

The Buddha's own life provides a prime example of his strong position in this regard. The widespread and firmly held belief at the time was that only members of the Brahmin caste could become spiritual leaders—but the Buddha, who belonged to the ruling caste, demonstrated the fallacy of this view by becoming one of the most successful spiritual teachers who ever lived. And he achieved that success with unshakable self-confidence, offering, before his eventual liberation, this clear expression of his determination:

> Let my flesh and blood dry up, leaving my skin, veins, and bones. Still, I shall not give up my effort until I achieve the highest level which can be won by human ability, human effort, and human action.[4]

This attitude strengthened the Buddha's mind for the final conquest of greed *(lobha)*, malice *(dosa)*, and illusion *(moha)*. With the development of unsurpassable wisdom and boundless feelings of generosity and compassion, he attained enlightenment, the highest level of inner purification. Having sat under a *bo* tree one night with firm determination and continued meditation, he stood up in the morning victorious and self-content.

Now he was emphasizing the same initial preparation—empowering the mind with firm determination—when talking to his ordained disciples about spiritual success and encouraging his lay disciples toward material success. Having cleansed the mind of fear and doubt, we can get into the real work with unsurpassed confidence: "You can succeed if you pursue your goal with confidence."

RIGHT EFFORT

The two stages of inner preparation—removal of inner barriers and enhancement of self-reliance—set the stage for worldly success. Now, with right effort, we have the perfect beginning for any successful endeavor.

The Buddha identified two characteristics of effort. First, effort alone makes inner preparation meaningful; inner preparation without effort is inadequate for success. The Buddha never promoted such views as "Just visualize it and wait; you will get it." Instead, the right thought should always be followed by right effort.

Next, effort means more than mere hard work. The Buddha's philosophy does not simply say "Work hard and you will achieve success." Instead, the Buddha emphasized the need to strive wisely and to achieve success methodically. Wise decisions and wise actions—not mere hard work—make the layperson's effort genuinely meaningful.

For anyone brimming with aspiration, this exemplifies the Buddha's implicit motto: "You can do it if you make the right effort."

FOUR STEPS TO WEALTH

In order for his lay disciples to reap the best results, the Buddha explained right effort in these four steps:

> What is the right effort [to succeed in secular life]? Suppose a certain person maintained his or her life with trading, cattle-farming, archery, government service, or any other profession or industry. That person develops knowledge and skills in the profession,

acquires organizational skills, does the necessary work at the right time, and shows strategic search for new means of improvement. This is what I call the right effort.[5]

Despite its brevity—possibly caused by the bhikkhus' summarizing a long speech for the sake of preserving it through memory—this definition of right effort is thorough by any standard. Notably, it indicates that wise decisions and right actions combine to lead an individual toward success. Its four steps are so important that each of them deserves a detailed discussion.

STEP 1: DEVELOP KNOWLEDGE AND SKILLS IN THE DESIRED PROFESSION OR BUSINESS

Acquisition of knowledge and skills in the relevant field is an essential part of right effort. The Pali term used in this context is *dakkho alam katum*, which means "improvement of abilities necessary for doing the work." *Dakkho* includes both knowledge and skill. These qualities provide a person with proficiency in his or her professional field. Consequently, the layperson learns to excel in whatever is undertaken. A trader, for instance, develops a thorough knowledge of his wholesale market and his resale profits, and thus become skilled in buying and selling.[6] Overall, possession of considerable knowledge and skill in the relevant field is necessary in order to strive correctly.

This improvement process should be initiated by parents during their offspring's childhood. In the *Sigalovada Sutta*, the Buddha noted that parents should take the initial responsibility for guiding children toward a suitable profession.[7] As they enter adulthood, children then take the responsibility for further enhancement of knowledge and skill.

In the modern context, education, job-related training, and business-related research and studies are all aspects of the same requirement. We are well aware that success in this competitive world depends on qualifications. Those who enjoy commanding positions in the modern workforce have gained masterly knowledge and superb skills, and thus they rapidly and steadily advance in business. This truth proves the Buddha's point that education and skill development are essential for those striving for success.

Modern psychology would identify this level of improvement as the "self-actualized stage" in skill development. Most people in any society acquire only the basic knowledge and skills of their respective fields. A small percentage, however, go beyond that to develop specialized knowledge and skills. The Buddha wanted his lay followers to actualize themselves in their professions. So, he recommended that better knowledge and skills are indispensable for initiating the march toward material success.

STEP 2: ORGANIZE WORK AND BUSINESS SKILLFULLY

Organizational skills are another significant prerequisite for anyone striving to advance in any field. The Buddha consistently emphasized the importance of organizing one's work and business. In the *Mangala Sutta,* he stated that having "organized work and business" is a blessing to the layperson.[8] The Pali term he used to mean organizational skill is *dakkho alam sanvi-dhatum,* "becoming genuinely skillful in organization."

Of course, organizational skill is a broad topic. In the Buddha's teachings, this skill includes both self-organization and work-related organization—and is useful for both initiating and successfully continuing any task. Here, we will pay close attention to the skills that are particularly important for the initial phase of an ambitious project, knowing that the same skills may also be applied at other stages of work and business.

The Buddha's own biography clearly evidences what he meant by organizational skill. After reaching the highest level of inner purification, he launched one of the most successful humanistic projects ever recorded in history, including a massive program to influence social thinking and change. One of the first steps he took for this purpose was organization.

Initially, the Buddha organized himself. His daily routine indicates this: his daily activities were organized into five sessions.[9] The first was the early morning session, which he used for his own meditation practices. Then, he allocated the morning session for visits to people who needed his help. During the afternoon session, he instructed his ordained disciples and any lay followers who visited him. Two night sessions were used for the guidance of ordained disciples' meditation practices and for the discussion of profound Dhamma topics. In this most systematic way, the Buddha organized his energetic life.

He also demonstrated amazing skills in organizing his new society and was the first social reformer to bring such systematic order to a social movement. First, he appointed Sariputta and Moggallana, two of his most qualified ordained disciples, as his chief leaders. He then offered titles to eighty bhikkhus and assigned them positions of leadership based on their knowledge and skill in their respective fields. Through his own leadership, the Buddha demonstrated how an organized effort would lead to amazing success.

In his advice to lay followers, the organization of the workforce drew the Buddha's special attention. He specifically mentioned that qualified persons should be appointed as leaders. "Giving leadership to a woman or a man who follows addictive habits and squanders wealth signifies decline," he stated.[10] As mentioned in the previous chapter, the leadership should assign employees work and duties befitting their skills and abilities. In addition, employers should offer their employees benefits, leaves of absence, and wholesome food.

This approach also contributes to the success of the business in a different way. When treated in this way, employees develop a very favorable attitude toward their employers. Consequently, they work to the best of their capabilities. "Commitment to the job, refraining from wrongdoing such as stealing, and appreciation of the employer" are some of the favorable results obtained from satisfied workers.[11] Such workers definitely contribute to the success of any business.

The Buddha also discussed the organization of small businesses, such as the home production of clothing made of cotton or wool—a widespread occupation during that time. He regarded this type of small business as family work, in which both husband and wife should share responsibilities. Interestingly, his idea that the wife should be in charge of organizing such a family-based business[12] emphasizes the Buddha's high regard of women's skill and intellectual strength.

Overall, the Buddha guided his ambitious lay followers to stay a systematic and organized course of action in order to achieve their objectives; and he offered them invaluable instructions on how to organize their work and businesses. This guidance is evidenced in both his life and teachings; and his organization of his own actions and plans indirectly cites himself as an example to follow.

STEP 3: COMPLETE THE NECESSARY TASKS AT THE RIGHT TIME

Timely action, from the Buddha's point of view, is one of the most crucial factors for secular success. This requirement, of course, relates to organization. Timely action is identified separately, however, because of its overwhelming importance in any endeavor. In discussion with King Kosala, the Buddha cited timing as the single most important factor for success in material life:

The most important factor for a person's development
is doing the action at the right time. A footprint of an
elephant can cover the footprint of any walking animal. Similarly, in its importance, timely action stands
out among all other actions.[13]

The Buddha warned that failing to act at the right time, one
would also "fail to acquire new wealth, and what one has
already acquired will soon diminish."[14]

To represent this overwhelmingly important requirement for
achievement, the Buddha used such words as *analasa* and *appamada*. Existent English translations, however, fail to convey the
broad meanings of these original Pali words. *Analasa* is generally translated as "not being lazy," while *appamada* is interpreted
as "heedfulness," or "diligence." Literally, these translations are
acceptable and point simply to hard work as a means to success. As the Buddha used them, however, they carry a more
profound meaning: they emphasize the importance of right
action at the right time. The "action" may be a laborious task
that demands both physical and mental energy, or the action
may be simply a decision or a step that needs a few minutes of
thinking.

Taking examples from everyday life, the Buddha explained that
some people lazily avoid and postpone work, blaming weather,
citing hunger or fullness, or saying it's too early or too late for
work.[15] Such examples show that the opposite of *analasa* is negligence, procrastination, or lethargic postponement of work, a
dangerous habit that clearly thwarts one's effort for success. Thus,
analasa signifies the use of physical energy at the right time.

In conversation with King Kosala, the Buddha used the word
appamada to mean "timely action."[16] "If you live your life doing
the right action without delay, you protect and save yourself,
your elephants, your wealth, and your storehouses," he said.[17]

He also mentioned in the same speech that King Kosala's timely actions would encourage his staff and employees to perform their own duties on time.

In general, well-timed actions, from the Buddha's viewpoint, make a layperson's endeavor for success profoundly meaningful. Failing to time actions properly when striving for wealth, one resembles "a weak heron near a dry pond."[18]

STEP 4: LOOK FOR STRATEGIC MEANS OF IMPROVEMENT
The other step to a layperson's material success, according to the Buddha, is to search for strategic means of improvement. This may be one of the most innovative and effective practices leading to individual success. In brief, it calls for introducing new concepts into professional and business fields, and applying new methods for the improvement of overall performance.

The technical Pali term is *upaya vimamsa. Upaya* means "strategic approach," or, functionally, "thinking out of the box," as opposed to the commonly accepted way of trying something. *Vimamsa* has several meanings, such as "examination" and "testing." Taken together as a technique for succeeding in lay life, *upaya vimamsa* means "strategic investigation of new means of improvement in professional and business fields"—a technique that may well be called "innovation."

The Buddha was aware of new developments in his society, particularly in the fields of business and trading. As noted in chapter 1, the sixth century B.C.E. was the emerging age of business in India, with altogether new innovations. Hundreds of carts from the states of Magadha and Kosala took merchandise to Gandhara to be transported to the Greek islands. Goods also reached the port of Barygaza, on the western coast of India, bound for the Western world via the Red Sea. New strategies had to be implemented in all these ventures, in order to protect, transport, sell, and exchange merchandise.

For instance, the Buddha's chief supporter Anathapindika, a business tycoon in Savatthi, formed a trade organization to collect and export merchandise to the West. Upali, another supporter of the Buddha, began the first known banking system. The Buddha's awareness of these new developments in trading and business may have persuaded him to encourage his lay followers to implement new methods for their material success.

Whatever the reason, with his suggestion of *upaya vimamsa*, the Buddha offered an invaluable piece of advice to his motivated lay followers: "Invent new concepts and strategies to steer your journey toward success." He himself practiced the same philosophy when he established and organized his new society within the traditional rigid society. And, of course, he achieved exceptional success in his own endeavor.

SUMMARY

The Buddha offered useful instructions to guide his lay followers' initial effort for prosperity. He first shaped their mentality and strengthened their mind. Next, he guided their effort, offering useful instructions to make it truly meaningful. The Buddha did not encourage his lay community to wait for a sudden fortune, a windfall such as a modern lottery win; and neither did he tolerate quick and easy money through whatever means. Instead, he helped his disciples to strive methodically and to establish themselves in life "just as ants build up their anthill."[19] In sum, according to the Buddha, new knowledge and the development of skills, organization, timely action, and innovative methods constitute the right effort for success.

CHAPTER 4: RETAINING WEALTH

The layperson's objective, "I should live a long and dignified life with my relatives and teachers with the
wealth obtained through rightful means," is pleasant,
agreeable, charming, and only achievable through
effort.

The Buddha, *The Numerical Discourses*

The Buddha observed two kinds of prosperous people:
those who attained prosperity but failed to retain it, and
those who became prosperous and secured their prosperity. "Some families obtain great wealth, but cannot hold on
to it for long,"[1] and later in the same sutta, he mentioned that
other families kept their prosperity undiminished. The Buddha
examined why and how some succeeded in retaining their prosperity while others failed. In most cases, he observed individual habits, characteristics, and behavior as contributory factors
in a person's steady progress or downfall. The Buddha readily
offered guidance to his wealthy lay disciples to enable them to
avoid disasters and to stabilize their achievement. He formu-
lated a set of principles that would specifically help his lay followers to retain their prosperity undiminished. This chapter
will put together and elaborate on these principles.

Importantly, we may look at the Buddha's philosophy of lay life to understand his guidance of laypersons toward stable success. Short-lived prosperity, he observed, is no success at all—and a layperson's aim should be not only to gain prosperity but also to maintain it. In striving for material success, one should strive for unfading affluence for life.[2]

Let us look at each of the Buddha's recommendations for retaining prosperity (focusing mainly on the *Vyagghapajja* and *Pattakamma Suttas* in the *Anguttara Nikaya,* and the *Sigalovada Sutta* in the *Digha Nikaya*).

STEP 1: TAKE ACTIONS TO PROTECT WEALTH

Protective actions are one of the most important requirements for safeguarding one's prosperity. "A layperson has obtained wealth through right effort, skill, and just means," the Buddha said. "He or she should take actions to protect it from the king, thieves, fire, water, and unfriendly relatives."[3]

The Buddha's definition of protection of prosperity reflects the threats encountered by the wealthy in his society. Close observation reveals that similar threats lurk in society today. Modern law allows personal wealth to be confiscated in certain circumstances by the government or taken over by financial institutions. Thieves—in both old and new forms—thrive in today's society; and fire and flood continue to damage city properties. After twenty-five centuries, people still experience the same threats to their wealth.

To guard wealth from governmental interference, the Buddha suggested acquiring it in the right way and fulfilling one's duties to the government. In guiding people to prosperity, he constantly reminded them that wealth must be acquired through just means. *Dhammikehi dhammaladdhehi* (using rightful means and acquired through harmless means)[4] was the phrase he always used to signify "just effort for material success." Through just means, a successful person reduces the risk of the government taking over his or her wealth.

The Buddha also taught that the individual and the government are bound together by duties and responsibilities. As previously noted, payment of taxes is the individual's primary duty toward the government. The Buddha used the word *rajabali* to refer to the portion of wealth an individual should give to the government.[5] By fulfilling these duties, the wealthy person dramatically diminishes if not eliminates the threat of takeover by the government.

During the Buddha's time, people protected their wealth from thieves by keeping it in their personal possession. Today, however, one leaves one's wealth with others, such as financial institutions. The fall of large institutions due to corruption and other reasons indicates the need to invest wealth wisely to protect it from modern-day thieves. For maximum protection in this situation, one can still follow the Buddha's teachings by choosing the most trustworthy institutions in which to deposit and invest one's money.

The Buddha also advised protecting wealth by taking action to safeguard it "from fire and water" (*aggito va udakato va*)[6]—by extension we can take this to mean taking precautions to protect against any other such natural disaster as well, and other similar unexpected tragedies.

Taking steps to safeguard wealth "from unfriendly relatives" (*appiyato dayadato*) is another protective action. This advice may have been more relevant in the Buddha's time, but we can hardly rule it out today. Some people, for example, loan substantial sums to relatives based on mere trust. However, the beneficiaries might betray all trust and never return the loan. In some cultures, parents and grandparents are most vulnerable to this danger, with adult children and in-laws squeezing wealth out of elderly relatives. These occurrences suggest that steps to protect wealth from unfriendly relatives are a genuine need for some people in today's society.

Overall, the Buddha strongly encouraged his lay community to take the necessary steps to protect their wealth. That protection is imperative for a person to enjoy lifelong prosperity. The Buddha's use of the term *arakkha sampada* identifies the protection of wealth and indicates its overwhelming importance: it is a phrase that means "to take steps to protect wealth is similar to fulfilling a notable accomplishment."

STEP 2: SELECT WISE AND UPRIGHT PEOPLE FOR COMPANIONSHIP AND CONSULTATION

The Buddha consistently reminded his followers that wise and upright people are an asset to the prosperous person and a shield to his or her prosperity. According to the Buddha's advice to the young man Dighajanu, such companions provide "future benefits and happiness" to those living a secular life "accepting gold and silver."[7]

Moreover, he counseled young Sigala on how association with undisciplined and morally corrupt people is a "channel through which wealth disappears."[8] Thus the Buddha, in his wisdom, discussed in detail how relationships can protect or destroy individual wealth.

The Buddha instructed his lay followers to keep in contact with qualified mentors, and to converse and especially to discuss ideas with them. In this way, they develop their personalities and gain knowledge and skills—which further enhances prosperity.

A mentor can be identified by four characteristics: discipline, inner development, mental strength, and wisdom. A mentor's use of language, reaction to tragic situations, and ideas expressed in discussion constantly shed light on his or her qualifications. By maintaining a long relationship with a mentor and reflecting thoughtfully on his or her behavior, one can decide whether he or she is qualified.[9]

Wise choice of close companions also plays a crucial role in the layperson's consolidation of success. The Buddha identified the significant roles that social, environmental, and peer influences play in our lives; and he vividly described the kind of companionship that leads to the decline of success.

For instance, some people may shower us with extravagant praise, but they offer very little help and anticipate too many advantages.[10] Others might be able to fulfill a request for help; but they apologize and decline saying, "Sorry, if you had asked me earlier, I'd have done it," or "Not now, perhaps in the future."[11] Some approve both our wholesome *and* unwholesome actions, praising us when we are in their presence but discrediting us at other times. And some might also entice the successful person to drink, gamble, and adopt similar harmful habits.[12]

The Buddha cautioned that the physical appearance of companions or their immediate display of impressive behavior does not offer enough or true evidence. To evaluate them, one needs to observe their behavior for a certain period of time, in order to know them correctly. And if one wishes for more prosperity, one should avoid "enemies in the guise of friends."[13]

Elaborating further, he described some salient characteristics of a genuine friend who would contribute to one's success. These include providing help in time of need, keeping secrets, retaining unchanged affection, and offering advice to correct harmful habits, such as drinking. Honest friendship between two persons may also be detected in their inclination to speak well of each other in the company of others.[14] Associating with friends who display these traits paves the way for a layperson to strengthen his or her success.

STEP 3: SPEND ACCORDING TO A FINANCIAL PLAN

In order to safeguard and enhance the success already achieved, the Buddha recommended that families and individuals have a financial plan. He specifically mentioned that a person with a high-class lifestyle despite achieving only a small income would soon diminish his or her wealth.

A financial plan guides the layperson to spend, invest, and save a portion of the income wisely. The Buddha emphasized the importance of such a plan and gave a clue to what he meant by "balanced spending":

> The wise layperson knows the amount of his or her income and expenses, and, with that knowledge, he or she calculates thus: "My income does not exceed my expenses, nor do my expenses make up too meager a portion of my total income."
>
> An experienced user of a scale [with two trays of equal weight hanging from the ends of the beam] knows, "If I put this or that weight on this tray, the other tray will rise or fall to this or that level." Similarly, the householder must know how to balance the amount of his or her expenses.[15]

As discussed in chapter 2, the Buddha suggested that a quarter of the total income is the right portion for personal use. The rest of the wealth is for investment and saving.

Significantly, these suggested restrictions are not meant to suppress a layperson's enjoyment of life. As discussed in chapter 1, the Buddha maintained that wealth should be used for one's own benefit and happiness; however, the percentage allocated for that use should be proportionate to one's income. Failure to honor this golden rule leads to numerous problems.

This advice is nowhere so useful than in modern society, where persuasion is working full force to entice every individual into an extravagant lifestyle. Alluring advertisements pound images of attractive cars, grand houses, and other enticing products into people's minds. So powerful is their appeal that an elegant lifestyle, through whatever means, has almost become the norm. Many people fall prey to such popular expectations; and social pressures cause many to lose patience with balanced spending.

Society, in general, respects people on the basis of their belongings: their vehicles, houses, and other material goods. Brainwashed by these social values, many people fail to adopt prudent financial plans. Instead, they use "easy" payment and monthly installment methods to purchase a plethora of items, at huge amounts of interest—adding to others' prosperity, while risking their own. Again, the Buddha's suggested financial plan can be immensely beneficial.

The Buddha observed that being free of loan payments is a great relief (anana sukha) for the layperson.[16] Dependence on loans to enjoy a lavish lifestyle is one of the biggest mistakes a layperson can make. The Buddha compared such a person to "a man who would pluck all the fruit from a tree to eat only what is ripe."[17]

STEP 4: TAKE STEPS FOR SELF-PROTECTION

The Buddha was also concerned about the dangers to a wealthy layperson's life and the lives of his or her family members. He specifically stated that using the wealth obtained through rightful means, "a wealthy person should take steps for self-defense, and should make life secure."[18]

The concept underlying these protective measures is that life is worth living happily and peacefully with family members. According to the Buddha's philosophy, a wealthy person should have a great expectation: "I must live a long life with my family members and teachers."[19] Precautionary actions would make this attainable.

Five factors may pose a threat to the personal safety and security of a wealthy person. They are fire, water, the law, thieves, and unfriendly relatives. The Buddha had already cited the same causes as potential dangers to one's wealth. He repeated these factors as possible threats to a prosperous person's life. He seemingly expected personal safety to be a major concern and self-protection to be necessary to prevent the dangers coming from these sources.[20]

According to the Buddha, "living at a suitable place" brings many benefits for a layperson.[21] On the one hand, the benefits can be spiritual; on the other hand, they can enhance personal safety. We assume that the Buddha advised his lay followers to avoid crime-infested neighborhoods, as well as areas prone to being "washed away by flood."[22]

He further noted that fear, danger, and misfortune all come from immature and opportunistic people (bala), and not from mature and virtuous people (pandita).[23] These remarks shed light on his advice to live in safe areas for protection: areas where natural dangers and human disturbances are minimal.

Protecting oneself and family members from punishment by the government is another important aspect of security. The entire family should respect the law of the land; and one's own actions—including one's livelihood—should cause no harm to society. He reiterated that wealth should be acquired lawfully, and that dutifulness to the government must be shown by paying taxes—as he stated whenever discussing the use of wealth. These steps are required to protect oneself and family members from the law.

Furthermore, to avoid tragic situations caused by criminals or accidents, the Buddha made a very simple but useful suggestion: "Do not travel at a dangerous time."[24] Someone who consistently "walks along streets at dangerous hours" risks his or her life and leaves family members in danger.[25]

Overall, the Buddha advised taking precautions against dangerous situations. This is the key to protecting oneself and one's family members—which is also protection of one's prosperity.

STEP 5: TAKE THE NECESSARY STEPS AT THE RIGHT TIME

This most important requirement for any kind of success appears over and over again. Chapter 3 has already drawn attention to how essential timing is to initiating any successful endeavor and maintaining prosperity.

As the Buddha saw it, timely action strengthens success in two ways. First, by removing disruptions, it steadies the progress already achieved. Second, timely action persuades others—coworkers, employees, and associates—to also act on time.[26] Advising King Kosala, the Buddha said that timely action would protect and increase his wealth. In the same discussion, he clarified that when the king followed the timing principle, others would do the same.

As noted previously, timely actions are the opposite of laziness, lethargy, negligence, procrastination, or any other word that suggests lack of desire, energy, or readiness to do what is necessary. To overcome physical and mental inaction means not only to stimulate success but also to steady it.

STEP 6: AVOID IMMODERATION IN ROMANTIC RELATIONSHIPS

In an extended simile, the Buddha compared wealth to the crystal waters of a beautiful pond. Engagement in multiple sexual relationships is a wide-open canal that removes the water from this pond and makes it empty. Avoidance of such relationships seals off the "canal" that drains wealth.[27]

Of course, the Buddha never intended to suppress the sex life of individuals; but he did advise his lay followers to be moderate, if they were to retain their success. And he used the term *itthidhutto* (becoming a woman-hunter) to suggest indulgence in sexual relationships. This term indicates a sort of addiction to romantic relationships: an addiction that, according to the Buddha, is a formidable threat to a successful person.

In the Buddha's own words, "whatever one earns dwindles away," with involvement in multiple sexual relationships.[28] Avoidance of such multiple connections contributes to the stability and improvement of one's prosperity.

STEP 7: REFRAIN FROM ADDICTION TO INTOXICANTS

Metaphorically, addiction to intoxicants is another "channel that pours out individual wealth."[29] Analyzing this problem, the Buddha noted that the side effects of this dangerous habit— sickness, bad reputation, shamelessness, mental disability, conflicts, legal problems—are the cause of ruin and pose a serious threat to one's prosperity.[30]

Our own society provides more than enough examples to illustrate this point. Health problems caused by drug abuse, smoking, and alcohol use are major killers today. A kidney or heart problem connected with alcoholism, or lung cancer stemming from smoking, could instantly reverse years of progress in one's life.

Bitter conflicts may arise in a family when one spouse becomes an alcoholic or a drug addict. Divorce and a child custody battle might follow, causing agony and financial loss. As a result, steady family progress experiences a severe blow.

On another note, the connection between drug or alcohol abuse and damaging legal problems seems necessary to mention. Obviously, alcoholism and drug addiction give rise to numerous risky practices, such as drunk driving and drug trafficking. These illegal practices lead to legal battles that could cause irreversible drawbacks. For a person who has just settled down in life, such problems are hardly tolerable.

Refraining from addiction to intoxicants such as alcohol, tobacco, and drugs removes some causes that rob us of success. It also paves the way for a mentally and physically vigorous life. In the Buddha's own words, non-addiction to intoxicants is an *ayamukha,* or "source of more prosperity."[31]

STEP 8: DO AWAY WITH GAMBLING HABITS

The other habit the Buddha saw as threatening to a person's success is compulsive gambling. This habit, according to his clarification, causes many negative consequences such as loss of friendship, confidence, and wealth; and much grief. He called this dangerous practice "a wide opening that drains wealth."[32]

The Buddha always opposed gambling, mainly because he always promoted human skill rather than individual luck as a means to success. To him, dependence on luck is a denial of the human ability to succeed. By choosing the wrong path, an addicted gambler ends up in a wilderness, rather than in the fortunate situation he or she dreams of.

The face of gambling has undergone many changes today. Lotteries, casinos, and online betting dominate organized and legalized forms of gambling. The negative consequences of compulsive gambling, however, have hardly changed. Even today, a habitual gambler will always lose wealth, lament over his or her financial failures, and fail to secure the trust and confidence of important people. Each of these negative effects plays its own role in dragging the person down the ladder of success.

By keeping oneself away from this dangerous habit, one blocks another "channel of dissipating wealth."[33]

STEP 9: AVOID IMMODERATE ENJOYMENT OF ENTERTAINMENT

Finally, the Buddha instructed his lay followers to avoid immoderate enjoyment of entertainment in order to keep their prosperity intact. He noted that a person who constantly watches "dancing, singing, music, plays, and performances" tends to experience a decline in his or her success.[34] The key word here is *abhicarano*, which means "more than usual visits" to festivities where all sorts of merrymaking are going on.

While the Buddha never asked his lay followers to abstain from entertainment, he did instruct them to know the limits of enjoyment. Exceeding these limits poses a threat to the progress already achieved.

The Buddha cited dancing, singing, music, storytelling, and musical performances as addictive types of entertainment for transitory satisfaction. Today, of course, "entertainment" comes in vastly modified forms. Outside the home, people find theaters, cinemas, playgrounds, nightclubs, and many other places of entertainment. At home, they have "entertainment centers," which provide multiple forms of "couch entertainment." In addition, there may be electronic media in each room for each family member's private enjoyment. All these sources of enjoyment can be included in the Buddha's definition of entertainment, and addiction to any of them undermines the progress one has already achieved in life.

While the Buddha's lay followers are entitled to find joy in entertainment, they are advised not to exceed the limits and obstruct their progress.

SUMMARY

Overall, the Buddha offered invaluable advice and guidance to his lay followers for strengthening and retaining undiminished success throughout their lives. He urged them to take steps to protect wealth, to consult and associate with wise people, to take timely action, to use wealth according to a plan, and to be concerned about self-protection. He also requested that they avoid indulgence in romantic relationships and entertainment, and abstain from intoxicants and gambling.

These guidelines suggest that professionalism, farsightedness, and behavior adjustment are the key factors for lifelong prosperity.

CHAPTER 5: THE BUDDHA'S VIEW ON RELATIONSHIPS

Neither their appearance nor a brief positive impression depicts a true picture of people.

The Buddha, *The Connected Discourses*

Careful selection of people for close relationships is immensely important in the Buddha's teachings for laypeople. In fact, he once advised his disciples to choose a solitary life, like that of a "lonely rhinoceros," if they failed to find suitable associates.[1]

The Buddha emphasized that the right choice of close associates is important because it contributes to peaceful and lasting relationships. To choose compatible people, he advised a process that consists of several steps. These steps are discussed widely throughout the *Sutta Pitaka*. They are brought together here for a comprehensive understanding of the Buddha's instructions on how to select close companions and associates.

These instructions do not mean to suggest we reject people as "unsuitable." The Buddha never asked his disciples to condemn an incompatible or even unpleasant or troublesome person. Instead, he advised them to understand that person's nature, to show compassion, and to provide an opportunity for improvement. Yet, compatibility is a dependable criterion for selecting individuals for close relationships. The Buddha's instructions are meant to facilitate this effort.

STEP 1: LEAVE ASIDE UNPROVEN TRADITIONAL CRITERIA

Traditional beliefs during the Buddha's time claimed race and caste to be the main criteria for selecting people for close ties, including marriage. Members of the Shudra caste, for instance, could maintain close links only with other Shudras. In marriage, in particular, they had to select only people of their own caste. The Buddha launched a tireless and fruitful campaign against these irrational beliefs. He once said that one should not even ask a person about his or her caste or race as a criterion to reject or accept that person.[2] And he encouraged his followers to leave aside race, caste, gender, and external appearance when selecting a person for a close relationship.

This clarification is important not only for finding companionship but also for selecting individuals for marriage. Caste, race, and other social differences should never be barriers for marriage or intimate relationships. And in discussing the elements of a successful marriage, the Buddha never advised lay disciples to select partners only from their own caste, race, or creed. Rather, compatibility in attitudes and behavior was one of the main factors he emphasized for a successful marital relationship.

Throughout his teachings, the Buddha stressed the danger of forming intimate relationships with a *bala*, or an inadequately developed and incompatible person.[3] A *pandita*, on the other hand, refers to a well-developed and compatible person. Such a person is recommended for a close relationship and can be selected from any caste, race, or social group irrespective of all differences. The Buddha always asserted that not birth but upright conduct and inner development determine a person's importance.[4]

Similarly, according to the Buddha's teaching, gender is no barrier to men and women maintaining any close association for a common goal. For instance, the Buddha's ordained male and female disciples maintained close relationships for the common goal of achieving self-purification and taking the Buddha's teachings to society.

The Buddha especially mentioned that female disciples should live close to male disciples for safety and counseling; and that male disciples should regularly visit and communicate with their female counterparts.[5] This association was based on the understanding of each person's objectives, rather than mutual attachment. Both sexes were advised to be mindful about their passion and to keep it in check.

In sum, the first step in selecting suitable close associates and forming intimate relationships is to disregard caste, class, race, creed, and similar attributes as a criterion. From the Buddha's point of view, these factors have no reason to justify their consideration.

STEP 2: BE CAUTIOUS ABOUT FIRST IMPRESSIONS AND INITIAL UNDERSTANDING OF PEOPLE

While the Buddha rejected traditional attitudes as criteria for selecting associates, he also discouraged reliance on first impressions and initial feelings. For example, some individuals may demonstrate great skill in presenting themselves as perfectly suitable for successful relationships. But we should refrain from leaping to the conclusion that their self-portrayal is a genuine reflection of their true nature. The following two stanzas spoken by the Buddha summarize this point:

> People cannot be known well by their appearance,
> Nor can they be trusted after a brief impression.
> Yes, the undisciplined may roam in the world
> In the attire of the well disciplined.

> Some adorn their unpleasantness
> With pretended suave action
> Like a clay earring or brass
> Painted with glittering gold.[6]

On the one hand, someone's appearance is not a dependable criterion for forming a genuine picture of them. The word used by the Buddha to suggest appearance is *vannarupa*, which means both "physical outlook" and "behavior." Both professional appearance and cultured behavior are included here as insufficient evidence for evaluating a person.

On the other hand, a brief association also fails to provide a clear understanding of someone. The Buddha used *ittaradassana*, which literally means "seeing little," to suggest a short association. A brief association may not reflect one's actual behavior and thinking because, for a short period of time, one may successfully conceal one's true nature.

Notably, however, this advice does not mean that those who are pleasant and courteous at the beginning of a relationship should be doubted—inherently pleasant people may immediately present themselves as such.

STEP 3: FOLLOW THE PROCESS OF ASSOCIATION, OBSERVATION, AND EVALUATION

While rejecting the insufficient criteria discussed above, the Buddha offered his followers a simple process for better understanding people—and thus better selecting compatible people for close companionship. This, in turn, would contribute to the construction of strong and healthy relationships. This simple process is as follows:

> Associate with a person for a certain period
> of time.

Observe and evaluate his or her words and
actions.[7]

The Buddha explained these steps to King Kosala when the
king, perhaps jokingly, introduced to the Buddha a group of
his secret agents posing as ascetics. King Kosala first respect-
fully greeted the spies in front of the Buddha. Then after they
left, he said to the Buddha, "Those ascetics have selected the
path for spiritual progress." The Buddha replied that the king's
judgment would be wrong because he (the king) did not possess enough evidence to support his claim.

"With a close relationship, you can [begin to] understand
others' discipline, purity, and wisdom," explained the Buddha.
"Still, the relationship should extend over a certain period of
time, not a short duration."[8] He emphatically stated that short-
term relationships are insufficient for gaining knowledge of
others.

People unfold themselves as time goes by; and we must associate with them and observe their behavior closely to better
understand their character's true nature. Then we may think
over and compare and contrast the behavior already observed.
To signify this process, the Buddha used the word *manasikaroti*,
which means to "ponder," "bear in mind," and "think over"—
and altogether, denotes "evaluation of behavior."

An important requirement for any accurate evaluation,
according to the Buddha, is wisdom. The Pali word used in this
context is *pannavata*, which means "by the person who uses
knowledge, skill, and wisdom." Evaluation should have a
rational basis. We may compare, contrast, and interpret the various forms of behavior we have observed; this allows us to
obtain a clear picture of this person whom we have known for
a certain period of time.

The importance of this evaluation lies in the conclusion that we need to find people with well-developed personalities with whom to establish close relationships. As stated in the previous chapter, the Buddha taught that all fears and worries come from inadequately developed people, not from people with wisdom.[9] Correct evaluation of behavior allows us to find wise people who cause no fear or worries.

STEP 4: CONSIDER COMPATIBILITY

The objective of the entire process of association, observation, and evaluation is to decide the person's suitability for a committed relationship. An issue here is compatibility. In order to maintain healthy relationships, the Buddha stated that closely connected people should be compatible.

The word "compatibility" does not, according to the Buddha, mean two persons belonging to the same caste, social class, or race; as already mentioned, he rejected these social truths as fragile and baseless. From his point of view, compatibility means the matching behavior and attitudes of two persons. Finding these similarities is the objective of the entire process of association, observation, and evaluation. He especially elaborated on the importance of compatibility for a successful marital relationship.

FOUR FACES OF COMPATIBILITY

Both partners can be pleasant to each other, the Buddha told us, when they have the following four similarities:

> Similar confidence in spiritual development
> Similar respect for self-discipline
> Similar respect for humanistic practices
> Similar level of wisdom.[10]

These similarities are so important for a peaceful marriage that close attention to each of them seems necessary.

SIMILAR CONFIDENCE IN SPIRITUAL DEVELOPMENT

To establish and maintain a healthy relationship, both partners should have similar beliefs about spiritual development (*ubho janapatiyo samasaddha*). This does not necessarily mean they should both follow a rigorous spiritual path. It does mean, however, that if one partner maintains strong respect for spiritual beliefs and practices, while the other holds them in total disregard, the two are simply incompatible.

SIMILAR RESPECT FOR SELF-DISCIPLINE

The next type of compatibility, according to the Buddha's observation, is both partners' similar regard for self-discipline (*samasila*). When one partner is well disciplined and the other unscrupulous, their incompatibility will become obvious and cause problems in the relationship.

Chapter 12 will present a thorough discussion of what the Buddha meant by "self-discipline" for the layperson. In brief, one's respect for such moral practices as not destroying life and not stealing are examples of self-discipline. If one is concerned about and skilled in self-discipline, so too should one's marital partner be. Such compatibility makes a relationship smooth and pleasant.

SIMILAR RESPECT FOR HUMANISTIC PRACTICES

Another sign of compatibility recognized by the Buddha is similar respect for humanistic practices. Some people are naturally self-centered while others are altruistic. A marriage in which the spouses belong to two different groups may be a mismatch, because of their incompatible attitudes and behavior.

According to the Buddha, humanistic practices or *dana*, also known as *caga* (generous acts), are the layperson's voluntary contribution to society. *Dana* is threefold: giving money and material objects; helping to protect life; and teaching and giving moral support, instructions, and guidance. One spouse's readiness and the other's reluctance to practice *dana* suggest clear incompatibility of the two persons.

SIMILAR LEVEL OF WISDOM

Various teachings of the Buddha suggest that "wisdom" conveys a broad meaning, which includes knowledge, skill, intellectual strength, emotional maturity, attitudinal improvement, and reasoning power. Similarities in these areas (*samapanna*) denote two partners' compatibility. This does not mean that both of them should have the same education, intellectual abilities, and so forth; it means that wide differences in these areas could cause incompatibility and lead to conflicts in the relationship. The Buddha implied that his lay disciples should be aware of this factor when selecting partners for marriage.

SUMMARY

The Buddha provided useful instructions to his lay community for selecting people for companionship and intimate relationships. He asserted that traditional, stereotypical attitudes about people would offer no clue to accepting or rejecting people for close ties. Similarly, intuition and first impressions are unreliable criteria for judging the compatibility of people. Instead, he suggested, associating with people and observing and evaluating their behavior allow us to decide on their suitability for close association. Selecting partners for marriage, in particular, should be based on mutual compatibility. A similar concern for spiritual development, self-discipline, and humanistic practices, along with a similar level of wisdom, defines the compatibility of two partners.

CHAPTER 6: ESTABLISHING A MARITAL PARTNERSHIP

> When both partners trust each other, use pleasant
> words to communicate with each other, have
> self-discipline, and maintain upright conduct,
> their progress increases, and pleasant life is born!
> The Buddha, *The Numerical Discourses*

Careful selection of companions is merely a prerequisite for healthy relationships; it only brings two compatible, mutually acceptable individuals together. The Buddha's wisdom shows us that for a marital relationship to run smoothly, it is essential for the attitudes and behavior of both partners to reach a standard of mutual satisfaction. This chapter will discuss this crucial requirement in detail and highlight its applicability to contemporary life.

From the Buddha's standpoint, a relationship between a man and a woman (or any other marital relationship) can be raised to the level of "a union between a god and a goddess."[1] This metaphor suggests the potential peacefulness and happiness inherent in such a relationship—and that, with developed attitudes and behavioral habits, both partners should be able to make their relationship blissful for each other.

DUTIES, OBLIGATIONS, AND RIGHTS

The Buddha observed that the fulfillment of duties and obligations is more persuasive in marriage than any fight for rights. Thus, he recommended dutifulness and obligation as powerful ways to establish a successful marital relationship.[2]

The philosophy goes as follows: when both persons are mindful of their duties and obligations, neither tends to misuse the other—thus the need to fight for rights rarely arises. Importantly, the Buddha did not identify this approach as a magic solution to all marital conflicts. He simply held that fulfillment of duties and obligations is an important step toward a blissful relationship between two partners.

What do "dutifulness" and "obligation" actually mean, as identified by the Buddha? He used several words, such as *upakara* and *paccupatthana*, to mean "dutifulness" and *paccupakara* and *anukampa* to denote "obligation." His definitions of these words have not been preserved; but his descriptions of their actions present a clear view of his meaning.

Dutifulness is the natural and selfless commitment associated with one's position in a relationship. As explained in the *Sigalovada Sutta*, parents' provision of help, care, food, and guidance to children can be taken as a clear example of duty. Dutifulness in a relationship is not dependent on the gratefulness of the other person; it is intrinsic to one's position in the relationship.

Obligation, as explained in the same sutta, means one's gratefulness to, or responsibility for, the other person who has fulfilled his or her own duty. For instance, "showing kindness to her husband" is an obligation of a wife when, through his words and deeds, her husband has shown respect to her. While duty is inherent in one's position in a relationship, obligation depends upon the other person's dutifulness in that relationship.

The Buddha believed that both duty and obligation strengthen the connection between two persons in relationship by making both individuals beneficial to each other. Balanced usefulness of one person to the other is the theme behind dutifulness and obligation. We notice that some marital partners fail to accomplish their duty and obligation, while still insisting on the other person's observation of the same. This approach—which may very well be called misuse or abuse—would certainly give rise to conflicts in a marital relationship.

Having stressed the importance of dutifulness and obligation in a successful union between a man and a woman, the Buddha also recommended five specific duties and obligations for each.[3] While some of these recommendations reflect the specific cultural values of the Buddha's society, we can nonetheless find timeless practicality and effectiveness within them, and can see ways in which the instructions to a husband and wife are largely universal.

FOR HIM

First, let us briefly focus on the five duties and obligations recommended for the male partner.

1. SHOW RESPECT TO HER

In the Buddha's era, men hardly paid attention to women's rights and dignity. At a time when wives were expected to please their husbands and raise the children, the Buddha made a revolutionary assertion: A man should show respect to his wife, in order to make the relationship happy and peaceful. The Pali word he used for "respect" is *sammananaya*, which means "with respect and admiration."

Importantly, this is the very first of the five duties the Buddha requested a husband to fulfill. He brought it to the forefront seemingly because of its overwhelming importance for a healthy

marital relationship. All other duties assigned to the male partner in a relationship seem secondary to respect. Whatever a
husband does for his female partner would be shallow and
worthless if he fails to do it with genuine respect for her.

Various teachings of the Buddha provide more details about
the respect that is so crucial to a healthy relationship. Importantly, respect should not be just a superficial verbal expression. Instead, respect must originate from within and become
known through words and deeds.

In a broader sense, loving-kindness symbolizes this kind of
respect. Feelings of genuine love and compassion should precede verbal and physical expressions of love. From the Buddha's
standpoint, the female partner deserves such respect from her
male partner. She is not the personal property of a husband
who would manipulate her at will; she is an equal and
respectable partner in the relationship.

2. REFRAIN FROM WORDS THAT MIGHT HURT HER

This habit is connected to the first one, since refraining from
the use of hurtful words is another way of showing respect.
Still, to ensure the consistency of a male partner's respectful
behavior toward his beloved, the Buddha asked him to follow
this principle closely. Instead of showering her with sweet
words when necessary and scolding her at other times, a husband must always be mindful of his words. He should not only
use pleasant words but also refrain from harsh words whenever
he communicates with her or talks about her to others. The
Buddha's phrase *avamananaya* indicates this requirement.

Throughout his public teachings, the Buddha maintained that
harshness never solves problems or brings people closer. This
seems particularly valid in marital relationships. Unpleasant
words would cause the wife to resist and to devalue her husband's
personality. The Buddha clearly touched upon the soft nature of

women and reminded husbands not to take advantage of it. Instead of trying to intimidate his wife with harsh behavior, a husband should adhere to a gentle pattern of communication. This will contribute to a pleasant relationship between the two.

3. PRACTICE FAITHFULNESS

A husband must first be mindful of his own faithfulness to his wife before he begins to inquire about her faithfulness to him. The word *anaticariyaya* indicates this necessity. The Buddha consistently reminded married men not to seduce women. And he used various techniques, including self-reflection and understanding, to discourage them from extramarital relationships:

> If a certain person seduces my wife, I would not tolerate that person. Similarly, if I seduce somebody else's wife, he will not like me, either. With this awareness, I must refrain from seducing women.[4]

A husband's introspection, understanding, and rational and ethical resolution enable him to remain faithful to his wife. While admitting impulsive sexual urge as the most powerful and predominant human desire,[5] the Buddha instructed men to handle it responsibly for the sake of their family life.

4. GIVE UP DOMINANCE

The Buddha persuaded men to give up dominance if they wished to maintain a blissful relationship with their female partners. His use of the Pali phrase *issariya vossagga* says it all. *Issariya* means "authority" or "power"; *vossagga* means "relaxation" or "relinquishment." Taken together, the two words refer to a man's "giving up of dominating behavior" in a marital relationship.

With this recommendation, the Buddha suggested a greatly effective means for men to strengthen their relationships with women. When men would still assert that they were the superior authority in their marriages, that they were "the person who makes decisions that wife must agree with," the Buddha claimed they must give up this mentality for the sake of a successful relationship.

A man's giving up of authority, on the other hand, does not mean the female partner makes all the decisions. The Buddha encouraged both partners to make decisions together and to follow these decisions harmoniously, instead of allowing one to dominate the other.

The Buddha said that a wife should never be her husband's puppet, nor should he be hers. On another occasion, he explained that a successful wife can be mother-like, sister-like, or friend-like.[6] This remark supports the Buddha's view that both partners in a marital relationship should share the authority in order to coexist peacefully.

5. RESPECT HER FONDNESS FOR BEAUTY

The Buddha identified women as admirers of beauty, and he encouraged men to respect their partners' penchant for beautiful things. The phrase *alankara anuppadana* indicates men's respect for their female partners' desire for beautiful objects. *Alankara* stands for anything attractive, such as pretty clothes and ornaments; *anuppadana* means "giving as a present." The Buddha remarked that men should provide their beloved partners with beautiful objects.

This duty reflects the best way for a man in that society to show his respect for his female partner's love of beauty. During the Buddha's time, women did not go shopping and select what they wanted to buy. Usually men visited the marketplaces, where they would buy the requirements for the entire household. In that social setting, women usually requested their male partners to bring home what they (women) wanted. A man's "giving of beautiful items" suggests his respect for his female partner's request. Because he uses family resources to purchase household necessities, he should also buy what his female partner would like to have.

What is important for today's relationships is the concept behind a man giving beautiful things to his beloved. He needs to understand that she is an admirer of beauty. While he might not mind driving a decade-old, rusty truck, she would prefer a beautiful new car. He might be satisfied with grass in the front yard; she would prefer flowers and ornamental plants in the garden. A male's respect for his female partner's appreciation of beauty is the rationale behind providing her with attractive things.

"These are the five treatments a husband should offer to his wife," the Buddha remarked after explaining these duties.[7] A man who expects to establish a mutually rewarding relationship must be mindful of these five duties toward his partner. The Buddha further noted that, thus treated, she will "feel compassion" toward him.[8] This feeling is the knot that connects her to him and keeps her love untarnished.

FOR HER

To match these five duties, the wife must also follow a course of action toward the partner who completes his own duties and responsibilities. Her successful association with her husband is also based on the concept of give-and-take, rather than a forceful insistence on rights.

1. WORK IN AN ORGANIZED WAY

A wife's organized approach to her work is seen by the Buddha to be useful in maintaining an excellent relationship with her husband. The Pali term used in this context is *susanvihita kammanta hoti*. This phrase does not clarify the *kind* of work she does; it simply means "[She] should have well-organized work"—thus encouraging her to be organized in whatever she does.

Obviously, cooking, housekeeping, and taking care of children, as well as supervising these activities, were an essential part of women's work during the time the Buddha was teaching. However, the Buddha never confined females to the chores at home. He was an unequivocal advocate for women's rights and freedom, and acknowledged that a woman's intellectual strength is equal to that of a man.[9]

Based on this fact, we may include in the Pali word *kammanta*, as referred to a woman's work, whatever task that "suits her skill and interest."

The Buddha was not concerned with the kind of work a wife does, but how she does it. While most female followers of the Buddha were housewives, some were landowners and home-business partners. Whatever a woman's occupation, the Buddha encouraged her to do it in an organized way. A woman's self-organization, he maintained, contributes to a peaceful relationship with her male partner.

2. HANDLE FAMILY RELATIONSHIPS

This duty of a wife basically reflects the Buddha's society. Since most men seeking the Buddha's guidance in secular matters were business people and property-owners, they would hardly be spending their daytime hours at home. Their wives, meanwhile, had ample time to communicate with relatives and friends, and to deal with household employees and other important people related to work or business. Considering this situation, the Buddha seems to have given instructions on family relationships to the female.

Today's world has changed drastically, however, and it would be difficult to assign the same duty specifically to a wife. Both husbands and wives may work; some husbands stay at home while their wives work. Today maintaining relationships with important people is a task that needs to be shared. Nevertheless, for many families, the wife seems to be the most qualified person to handle relationships with others. While most men prefer to be introverted, women seem to have a natural inclination and knack for such relationships. Women's interests and skills in relationships place them ahead of men to handle family relationships with others. Thus, the Buddha's remark that a wife should monitor family relationships with outside people seems relevant even today.

3. BE FAITHFUL

The Buddha emphasized that, like a faithful husband, a wife should be faithful as well. Heeding this principle, which emphasizes abstinence from extramarital relationships, further enhances the relationship between a man and a woman.

Again, the Buddha never allowed men to use women as their personal property. A husband has no extra privilege to have more than one sexual relationship, while forcing his wife to have only him. Abstinence from sexual misbehavior applies equally to both. As long as a husband remains faithful and fulfills his duties toward his wife, she has an obligation to be faithful to him. As we will see in chapter 12, should a husband no longer carry out those duties and responsibilities, his wife should have the right to make her own decision.

4. TAKE STEPS TO PROTECT FAMILY WEALTH

The Buddha portrayed men as susceptible to harmful social forces. As indicated in several suttas, men may become victims of money-wasting habits such as alcoholism, gambling, and unsuitable relationships (though of course these problems can equally afflict women). The Buddha taught that it is the wife's responsibility to protect family wealth—and her actions in this regard would strengthen her relationship with her husband.

Specifically, the Buddha said that a wife "should not swindle, save greedily, or waste away the wealth, but protect it."[10] One way to do this is to regard it as "family wealth," rather than using or keeping it as her personal wealth. She should also know how to use wealth moderately, avoiding the two extremes of hoarding or squandering.

These steps seem to improve relationships in two ways. First, her honesty with family wealth increases his trust in her. Second, her judicious spending wins his respect. Both reactions enhance the unity and togetherness of the relationship.

5. SHOW SKILL AND ENERGY

"Skillfulness and energetic engagement in everything she does" is the next duty that a wife needs to fulfill to maintain a successful relationship with her husband.[11] The Buddha did not explain—or the suttas did not preserve—what "everything" (sabba kicca) might mean. But it was undoubtedly not servile duties at home.

As an equal partner in the relationship, a woman was expected, according to her skills and interests, to perform an active and responsible role in the family. Organizing a family business, maintaining relationships with others, protecting family wealth, and sharing the duties of raising children— these are some of the activities that may require her skill and energy.

Her energetic and skilful fulfillment of these duties enhances her relationship with her partner, because in this way she becomes an active participant in family success. When both partners work toward a common goal, they tend to please each other.

6. PLAY AN ACTIVE ROLE AS HIS COMPANION AND GUIDE

In addition to the five duties that appear in the *Sigalovada Sutta*, the Buddha advised that a woman who plays an active role as her husband's companion and guide can also become a successful wife.

Although some successful wives regard themselves as followers, this attitude is not essential for a happy marriage. A wife can be the provider of love, guidance, and companionship.[12] Some wives love and care about their husbands just as a mother attends to a child. Some show the right path to their husbands, just as an elder sister does to a younger brother. Others regard their husbands as mutual friends and equal partners. These attitudes and behaviors contribute immensely to the success of a marital relationship.[13]

Thus the Buddha's remarks suggest that a wife should share the responsibilities of the family equally with her husband. While he recommended that a wife should refrain from acts that demean her husband, he never said that only submissive women become successful wives. Instead, women who play active roles as mentors, guides, and equal partners with their husbands contribute to the success of a marriage.

SUMMARY

The Buddha offered useful tips for husbands and wives to establish healthy relationships in which both mates enjoy love, respect, and dignity. As an overall element of healthy personal relationships, he called attention to the fulfillment of individual duties and obligations, rather than individual rights. He suggested that moral duties, such as faithfulness, provide immense psychological satisfaction for both partners. And a balanced distribution of power and sharing of activities and responsibilities certainly make each of them feel important in the relationship. These feelings, in turn, make both partners pleasing to one another.

CHAPTER 7: BEING PROUD PARENTS

"Creator" is a synonym for a parent. "First mentor" and "the beloved" are the other synonyms for a parent. These synonyms are relevant because parents bring children into the world, provide them with manifold help, feed and care for them, and teach them the right path.

The Buddha, *The Numerical Discourses*

People often asked the Buddha questions about parenthood. They wanted to know the most effective ways to raise children, the duties of parents, and techniques for maintaining healthy relationships with their children. "Sir, we are laypersons who live with children," some said. "Will you explain to us the right teaching that is beneficial to us?"[1] Others complained about their children's misbehavior and lack of respect, imploring the Buddha's help to correct the children and restore the relationships.[2] Listening to these requests and complaints attentively, the Buddha offered his guidance. This chapter discusses his tips for enabling mothers and fathers to become special, successful parents.

LOVING AND CARING FOR CHILDREN

Parental love and care, according to the Buddha, is a basic requirement for successful parenthood. Merely providing a child with nourishment and protection, however, does not make a father or mother an exemplary parent. These are only steps on the right path—and an inherent practice of honorable human beings.

The Buddha taught that proper use of a layperson's wealth should include allocation of money for the happiness and comfort of any children that person may have. One who refuses to use one's wealth for the care of one's own children is a "wicked person" (asappurisa).[3] These remarks suggest that feeding and caring for children is a minimum requirement for all parents, not a valid reason to consider themselves excellent parents.

In his advice to Sigala, the Buddha suggested that while being a parent does mean providing one's children with all kinds of physical care and attention, becoming a better parent means thinking beyond their physical comfort and protection. In the Mangala Sutta he cited "caring for children" (putta sangaha) as a "blissful sign" for lay life,[4] or an indication of future progress for both parents and children. And related speeches indicate that "caring for" children goes beyond concern for their physical well-being.

For the Buddha, raising a child means helping that baby become a great human being. Parents must make it a goal to help their children achieve inner development, knowledge and skill, and success in life. To triumph in this effort is to realize the fullest potential of parenthood.

FIVE DUTIES FOR PARENTS

Elaborating on the relationship between parents and children, the Buddha assigned five duties to parents.[5] Fulfilling these duties provides a tremendous opportunity for parents not only to establish healthy relationships with their children, but also to feel proud about themselves.

1. HELP CHILDREN REFRAIN FROM UNWHOLESOME CONDUCT

Parents are "the first teachers" of their children. The Buddha used the term *papa nivarenti* to mean the parental duty of keeping children away from unwholesome conduct. *Papa* means any wrong action done through words, deeds, and thoughts. *Nivarenti* suggests the effort to avoid such actions. Helping children to refrain from unwholesome acts is a part of parental teaching.

How can parents take steps to block the causes that would drag their children into unwholesome acts? The Buddha did not believe that a forceful approach, such as physical punishment, would help toward this end. "Everybody is threatened by punishment," he once said, discouraging any form of punishment.[6] In the *Sutta Pitaka*, we do not find a single instance of support for punishment as an effective way to mold children's behavior. Contrary to the belief in "spoiling the child by sparing the rod," the compassionate Buddha suggested better ways to help children to shape their behavior—these will be explored below.

He never recommended verbal abuse either as an effective way to help children to eliminate unwholesome conduct. Speaking in general on harsh language, the Buddha noted that an angry reaction would surely be the result of using such language.[7] Harsh words, he went on to say in the same verse, only cause frustration and agony for the speaker. From this point of view, verbal abuse, like physical punishment, would only prevent parents from influencing their children to depart from wrongful conduct.

Advising is a useful step to prevent children from adopting harmful practices. But parents must first hold themselves as an example: "One needs to place oneself at the suitable place before one instructs others. Such an adviser does not fall from grace."[8] To be successful advisers, parents must follow their own advice. When parents themselves abstain from harmful actions, they will succeed in persuading their children to abstain from similar actions.

Keeping children away from close companionship with corrupt and immoral friends is, according to the Buddha, another way to prevent them from getting used to unwholesome behavior.

The Buddha's advice to Sigala—a young boy who had just lost his father and was in a confused state of mind facing the challenges ahead—indicates how he would have any parent guide his or her children.[9] In particular, the Buddha told young Sigala not to maintain close links with morally corrupt people, because such relationships would ruin the young man's future. Discouraging children from having close connections with immoral people prevents children from getting accustomed to similar habits.

Overall, taking steps to prevent children from becoming corrupt and immoral is a primary duty of parents, according to the Buddha. Instead of leaving it to teachers and priests, parents themselves should show concern and take responsibility for the prevention of their children from learning personally and socially harmful habits.

2. LEAD CHILDREN TO WHOLESOME CONDUCT

In addition to taking steps to prevent children from getting used to unwholesome actions, parental duties include guiding children toward wholesome actions. The Pali term used by the Buddha is *kalyane nivesenti. Kalyane* means "actions that are beautiful, charming, and virtuous." *Nivesenti* means "establish in" or "be the cause of."

"Wholesome conduct" refers to words, deeds, and thoughts that are motivated by generosity, compassion, and wisdom. The components of wholesome conduct, therefore, are the practices of charity (*dana*), self-discipline (*sila*), and development of the mind (*bhavana*). The Buddha encouraged parents to implant these thoughts and actions in their children. With parents' dedicated commitment, children can acquire these qualities.

Again, parents must follow a right way of living in order for their children to select a similar path. Next, they should be aware of who their children's close companions are. The Buddha repeatedly stressed that association with *pandita* (virtuous and wise people) enriches our own characters; therefore, parents should persuade their children to keep company with such friends. And, again, he emphasized skillful communication as an effective technique for responsible people to instill wholesome behavior in others. The same emphasis applies to parents who are striving to lead their children to wholesome actions.

Nevertheless, the Buddha saw that we cannot always bring immediate happiness to someone, while trying to lead that person toward wholesome actions. Parents, in particular, find it difficult to please their children with the right advice. Children like to do whatever brings them immediate satisfaction rather than long-term benefits. They may feel annoyed to hear that what their parents want them to do is the opposite of what they wish to do.

On such occasions, the Buddha asked parents to stand by their values assertively and not give in. When parents are convinced they're taking the right steps for the child's personality development, they must follow these steps without hesitation. These assertive actions may upset the child, but in the long run they will bring about wholesome effects.

Prince Abhaya, who was holding a baby in his arms, asked the Buddha if he would ever use harsh words to influence someone's behavior.[10] In response, the Buddha said he would use only pleasant words, at the right time. However, he also indicated that when he knew a certain step to be right, he never hesitated to take it.

"Suppose something got stuck in this baby's throat," he continued. "What would you do?" Abhaya replied that he would somehow take it out. "What about the bleeding and the pain?" the Buddha asked. Abhaya said he wouldn't care, because his immediate concern was to save the child's life. The Buddha explained that certain actions are necessary to lead someone in the right direction, even though such actions might not please the person immediately. This example shows that, in their effort to lead children toward wholesome conduct, parents may use emphatic words rather than harsh language, and take steps despite their children's reluctance to follow those steps.

The Buddha's own life provides one of the best examples of how a father should commit himself to implanting wholesomeness in a child's mind. His own son Rahula was just seven years old when the Buddha promised him "a father's best gift." Having made Rahula a member of the Sangha, the Buddha took great care to assist in his personality development. The *Sutta Pitaka* has preserved several speeches addressed to his son, showing the Buddha's great concern about Rahula's acquisition of wholesome qualities and personality development.

Instead of giving orders, the Buddha often appealed to Rahula's rational thinking. "What is the purpose of a mirror, Rahula?" he once asked his little son. "To see one's own reflection," Rahula replied. "Similarly one's mind is to reflect on actions," the Buddha continued. "You need to evaluate your actions in terms of their consequences. Whatever brings about unwholesome effects for yourself and others, you should prevent yourself from doing it. If it causes wholesome effects, you may do it."[11] This is an example of the effective steps a father may take to instill upright conduct in a child's mind. The Buddha's guidance was so perfect that Rahula earned the title "one who is most willing to be trained."

By word and by deed, the Buddha conveys the message that parents should direct their children toward upright conduct. It is parents' duty to encourage their children to speak wholesome words, to do wholesome deeds, and to develop wholesome thoughts. This guidance should be parents' main objective, not merely a peripheral matter.

3. EDUCATE CHILDREN FOR A PROFESSION

The next parental duty, according to the *Sigalovada Sutta*, is to provide children with the proper education for a profession. This need was called *sippam sikkhapeti. Sippa* means "knowledge and skill necessary for a profession"; *sikkhapeti* means to "teach and educate." In this, parents may help their children directly and also seek the help of qualified people.

This duty signifies that parents should essentially take steps to improve their children's quality of life, besides helping their personality development. In the *Mangala Sutta*, the Buddha said, "Vast knowledge, skill, discipline, and pleasant words are great blessings."[12] "Discipline" and "pleasant words" suggest character development; "vast knowledge" and "skill" indicate professional qualifications. Children need their parents' help in both areas.

Parents during the Buddha's time had very few choices when preparing their children for a profession. They could provide their children with their own knowledge, or they might leave their children with qualified people. Well-to-do families sent their children to such places as Taxila, the capital of Gandhara and location of the world's first known academic institution. Today, however, parents have a wide range of opportunities for help with their children's education. Sending children to schools and colleges, and monitoring and spending money on their education, are some of the ways parents can prepare children for a profession.

The three parental duties discussed so far suggest that the aim of parents is to guide a child toward becoming a complete person. Character adjustment, knowledge, and skill development indicate completeness. More specifically, departure from unwholesome conduct and the acquisition of noble qualities improve a child's inner development. And then advancement in knowledge and skill makes the child a professionally capable person. The Buddha urged parents to make a committed effort to lead a child toward this end.

4. HELP CHILDREN SELECT SUITABLE PARTNERS FOR MARRIAGE

During the Buddha's time, parental involvement in finding partners for children seemed most appropriate. On one hand, without an organized educational system for all, the young generation failed to select partners wisely. On the other hand, without established marital law, marriage partners left each other without taking any responsibility for their children or abandoned partners. Against this social background, the Buddha asked parents to select suitable partners for their children.

Today we might argue that this parental duty is no longer important, that parents should allow their children to select their own partners. However, parental guidance can still be a useful contribution to children selecting partners. Without valuable experience, they may leap to the conclusion that a person's physical attractiveness is the sole criterion for a marriage partner. Soon after, they may realize how blind they had been. They then learn that more important factors, such as their partners' attitudinal improvement and emotional maturity, deserve careful attention before deciding to get married.

Parental guidance can help young adults to select their partners wisely and, consequently, to minimize conflict in their marital relationships. Their own marriages have already taught parents important lessons. They know that each partner's personality development plays a crucial role in making a partnership successful. Parents can pass such vital insight on to their children. Without needing to select their adult children's marriage partners, they can enlighten their children about making the right choice.

Marriage is the single most important step in a child's life. Parental guidance can enrich his or her knowledge about selecting the right partner. And so parents have reason to be proud if they can help their children at this crucial juncture—and the Buddha's advice seems just as practical, even today.

5. TRANSFER THE APPROPRIATE MEASURE OF FAMILY WEALTH TO CHILDREN AT THE RIGHT TIME

Finally, the Buddha asked parents to hand over. Of course, the Buddha did not suggest that parents hand over everything to their children and become homeless in their later years. Instead, he suggested that they transfer a portion of family wealth to children at the right time. A look at the Buddha's own words clarifies this. He used the word *dayajjam* to mean the family wealth that children deserve. This word means "a portion of wealth to be given as a parental gift to children." The other key word is *samaye,* which means "the right time."

This final step suggests the completion of parental dutifulness. Having been the inspiring guide of their children's personality development and material success, parents now complete their duty in style. They hand over the wealth to their children in appropriate proportions. After writing their last will, many parents live a relaxed life justified in thinking, "We have fully completed our duty and achieved the utmost success as parents."

SUMMARY

The Buddha guided his lay followers toward becoming the happy and successful parents of well-developed children. They guide their children's character development and education. They enhance their children's understanding of marriage and family life. Finally, they hand over an appropriate portion of family wealth to children at the right time. In thinking over one's achievement as a parent, one derives great happiness from it. Such dutifulness contributes to excellent relationships between parents and children. The Buddha remarked that children show their humble gratitude to parents when parents have fulfilled their duties toward them. These positive end results make dutiful parenthood greatly meaningful.

CHAPTER 8: DEALING WITH CONFLICT

When you talk to others, you may place yourself in the following five positions: I will speak at the right time; I will present facts; I will use soft language; I will speak for the listener's benefit; I will talk with compassion.

Sariputta, *The Numerical Discourses*

Solving interpersonal conflicts was as important to the Buddha as establishing successful relationships. Since his newly formed society consisted of men and women from all social categories, marked personality differences existed within that society and interpersonal conflict inevitably emerged.

With clear vision, the Buddha offered valuable support in solving and even preventing such conflicts. While his instructions were addressed to his ordained disciples, they were meant for the lay community as well. This chapter discusses his methods, which, even now, are greatly effective.

FIVE STEPS TO SKILLFUL COMMUNICATION

A remarkably fruitful approach to dealing with interpersonal conflict was introduced by the Buddha and explained by his chief disciple, Sariputta.[1]

According to this method, five communication skills bring about numerous positive effects. As Sariputta explained, failure to follow these guidelines brings about negative consequences and is cause for regret—and for speakers, most likely, meeting with resistance from their listeners. Let's look closely at the five communication skills that the Buddha and Sariputta regarded as essential for handling the conflicts of daily life.

STEP 1: ADDRESS THE MATTER AT THE RIGHT TIME

Timing was crucial in the Buddha's communication. He identified himself as a "speaker at the right time," and repeatedly stressed that the success or failure of any effort to communicate depends largely on timing.[2] Nobody, for instance, could "roll back the Buddha's Dhamma Wheel" (disturb the spreading of Dhamma), since "the Buddha knew the right time to speak."[3] Sariputta's elaboration on timing reiterates this idea: timing is crucial to solving interpersonal conflicts.

According to recorded evidence, the Buddha was the first to emphasize timing as an important factor in speech. This was in the sixth century B.C.E. The pre-Socratic Greek thinker, Protagoras, mentioned this concept for the first time in Western history in the fourth century B.C.E. And following him, Isocrates claims that timing (or *kairos* in Greek) is the most important requirement for persuasion—at least a half-century after the Buddhist tradition observed the effectiveness of this practice.

The meaning of the Buddha's "right time for communication" is broad. The first important consideration is the listener's relaxed mental state. The Buddha's conversation with Gotami, whose only child had recently died, indicates the importance of this factor.[4] Gotami took her little son to many doctors expecting a cure, but everybody gave her the same answer, that the child was dead and nothing could bring the child back. Frustrated and distressed, she eventually visited the Buddha, who was considered to be "the greatest of doctors," and implored him the child's health. Realizing Gotami's distress, the Buddha decided not to tell her the truth right away, and instead sent her to bring back a handful of mustard seeds from a household that had not known death. Because he knew she would resist and suffer upon hearing it, he waited for the right time to tell her the unpleasant truth that death is universal, inevitable, and unalterable—and in so doing, helped her lessen the pain and gain wisdom.

Psychologists confirm that a person in an unhappy mood is less likely to listen. A teen who has just brought home an average school report may protest vehemently if a parent advises making a better effort next time. A husband or wife who comes home after a confrontation with the team leader at work may find a spouse's grumbling more than irritating. Communicating when the listener is in a happier mood may yield better results.

The listener's physical well-being must also be attended to in timing a communication. The Buddha requested that his disciples first feed a man who, despite being hungry, was eager to listen to the Buddha.[5] The Buddha was aware that a conversation with a hungry man would bring lesser benefit. And before talking to an ordained disciple about the Dhamma, the Buddha first tended to his painful skin disease.[6] Obviously, a sound physical condition is required for the listener's mental well-being; and so the "right time" signifies a time when the listener is also physically well and fit.

The objective is to bring happiness and benefit to both the listener and the speaker. Waiting for the right time to communicate does not mean looking for the best opportunity to manipulate the listener. The presence of selfish or exploitive motives clearly contradicts the Buddha's teaching. He repeatedly stressed that the speaker should be motivated by loving-kindness and compassion, and not at all by opportunistic motives.

Choosing the most appropriate time to speak is a very powerful communication skill for solving or reducing interpersonal conflicts.

STEP 2: SPEAK ABOUT FACTS

The Buddha further stated that refraining from false accusation is another step to improving communication and reducing conflict in any relationship. As Sariputta suggested, what the speaker should bear in mind is this: "I shall speak about what has happened, not about what has not happened."[7] This skill also includes refraining from exaggeration or amplification of the listener's mistakes and weaknesses, and other forms of false accusation.

From a psychological viewpoint, we may exaggerate a person's weaknesses or mistakes mainly to gain his or her attention or to express our own anger. In an effort to emphasize proper care for a baby, a wife might tell her husband, "The child got the flu because you didn't cover him properly." Trying to vent his anger, the husband might retort, "You always say the stupidest things." In the first case, what has actually happened is that the child has fallen sick with flu; the given reason is a mere assumption. Secondly, the husband's statement is a sweeping generalization; he makes a general claim out of a single example. Both statements are amplifications. Both persons fail to say exactly "what has happened."

Exaggeration manifests in different forms on a daily basis. A mother who sees a plate slipping through her daughter's hands might scream, "You never hold on to anything." A wife who reads her husband's annual checkup report might say, "You don't exercise. That's why your cholesterol is high." These statements all expand, magnify, or add assumptions to what the speaker has observed.

People often speak in this manner because such language

seems soothing, somehow, to the speaker—though not, of course, to the hearer! Perhaps a person can relieve his or her emotional tension by directing a verbal attack toward the person causing that tension. The most probable repercussion, however, is the increased stubbornness of the listener, who might regard the speaker's words as false accusation or insult. Such a reaction hardly contributes to a healthy relationship between the speaker and listener.

The Buddha suggested presenting the facts without attaching our own meanings to them. Then we're in a better position to solve conflicts amicably. While people find it difficult to deny facts, they often welcome assumptions as a means to resist conflict resolution. What has happened has happened. For the sake of the relationship, the best approach is to take steps to prevent conflict from happening again.

This step does not mean that just because something is a fact, we must always speak about it to the person concerned. The Buddha said, "Even if something is true, I do not speak the truth when it is not agreeable to the listener."[8] Some truths serve no valid purpose, and so talking about them may be useless. To bring about positive change in our companion's attitudes and behavior, however, we must concentrate on facts and not assumptions.

STEP 3: USE SOFT LANGUAGE

The use of soft language, according to Sariputta, is another important aspect of successful communication when dealing with interpersonal conflict. Sariputta stated that the speaker should make a firm determination about the use of language: "I should use soft words, not harsh, rough words." Abstaining from the use of harsh language is, in fact, one of the eight precepts for a lay Buddhist. This emphasis highlights the crucial role words play in our everyday relationships.

"Using soft language," as presented in the Buddha's teaching, also conveys a broad meaning. It includes everything related to language, such as appropriate words, phrases, tone, style of speech, and pitch. The recurrent phrases *pharusavaca pativirato* (avoidance of harsh words) and *piya vaca* (pleasant words) refer to the very softness of the words themselves. The phrases *piyam vada* (speak pleasantly) and *snehena vakkami na parusena* (speak nicely, not harshly) suggest a pleasant tone and style of communication.

From the Buddha's viewpoint, when we use rough language to solve a conflict, illusion and anger dominate our minds. Believing that roughness will facilitate the listener's understanding springs from illusion. The truth is that harsh language inevitably provokes the listener to resist and rebel. Some people believe that by silencing the listener with harsh words, they have succeeded in persuading the listener to accept their suggestions. A child who remains wordless and grim after a parent's scolding may present this false impression. But in truth, the child's silence can indicate strong resistance and the parent's failure to convince. The use of rough language may seem to give immense satisfaction temporarily, but it will never help solve a conflict.

Modern psychology explains that anger, the other forceful factor behind harsh language, is a reaction to situations that appear threatening. Using angry words is a technique to destroy the source of a threat, not to resolve a conflict. Angry language, tone, or style suggests an attack. The impression that the speaker is attacking with words is the worst feeling he or she can communicate to the listener. Most people do not tolerate an attack; they defend themselves or counterattack. Anger-dominated harshness will rarely yield success in resolving interpersonal conflict.

Some might believe that the use of soft language reflects weakness, which a listener might take advantage of. This misunderstanding arises when softness is misinterpreted as power-lessness and timidity. The use of soft language, however, does not mean this. The Buddha constantly used soft words, but he also found emphatic language essential. Violent verbal outburst is at one extreme; powerlessness in speech is at the other. The Buddha indicated that we can avoid both extremes and still use emphatic words to deal with interpersonal conflict effectively.

In the *Dhammapada*, the Buddha mentioned that one should avoid words spoken in anger and rather speak disciplined words.[9] Such behavior prepares an environment that is receptive to solving the conflicts that arise in our everyday life.

STEP 4: SPEAK WITH THE FOCUS ON THE POSITIVE EFFECTS OF THE SOLUTION

Sariputta further explained that the speaker needs to focus on the positive side of the suggested solution. That focus can yield great results in resolving a conflict between two closely related persons. As Sariputta instructed, the speaker needs to bear in mind, "I will speak for the benefit of the listener." This attitude of the speaker highlights two points. First, he or she should have a clear understanding about the positive consequences of the solution. Next, the speaker should essentially explain to the listener the positive effects of the solution.

This approach to conflict resolution indicates that mere criticism without a plan to help the listener will fail to resolve a conflict between two persons. Some may tend to find fault with their associates just for the sake of criticism. Recognizing this harmful habit, the Buddha said, "If a certain person always criticizes a companion, that act does not show genuine friendship."[10] When the listener detects the speaker's motive, the listener instinctively tends to reject the speaker's comments. With a productive plan beforehand, the speaker can encourage the listener to be attentive.

The speaker's clarification of the positive effects of the solution further persuades the listener to accept the suggested solution. The speaker needs to explain to the listener why the problem at hand needs a solution, and how that solution would benefit the listener. Many listeners may tend to misinterpret constructive criticism when the speakers fail to clarify their objective. The misunderstanding arises because the speaker did not indicate the positive effects of his or her suggestion.

STEP 5: SPEAK WITH GENUINE COMPASSION FOR THE LISTENER

Finally, a compassionate attitude should dominate the entire process of communication. One who intends to solve interpersonal conflicts successfully should derive ideas, suggestions, and solutions from a compassionate heart. The speaker should make the following determination: "I should speak with a compassionate mind, not with an angry mind."[11]

The four requirements discussed in this section so far—timing, speaking about the facts, using language skillfully, and focusing on the benefits to the listener—are all rhetorical methods which are external. The compassionate attitude is the humanistic feeling, which is internal and, of course, essential.

In modern persuasive techniques, experts tend to focus mostly on the modification of external behavior. They ask us to show professionalism, or to follow certain steps that would touch the listener. For instance, we are told to listen and say "Sorry to hear about that" when someone relates a sad personal experience. The Buddha went a significant step further. He wanted us to feel in accordance with what we say.

External rhetorical methods of persuasion are essential but probably inadequate techniques to modify the behavior of an individual. The danger lies in the possibility that the listener might sense the speaker's lack of feelings. The verbal message

"I love and care about you, and that is why I want you to improve" contains great power to influence a person—but the nonverbal reality is much more significant.

We sometimes need to question ourselves about our own true intention when we communicate with others about their unskillful actions. Do we actually possess caring feelings to help them, or is something else at play? Why does a husband or a wife, for instance, always remind the spouse about a certain mistake she or he made in the past? Why do we constantly try to "correct" a certain person? These things warrant careful investigation. An action will be meaningful and fruitful if it is motivated by true compassion.

EXCEPTIONS TO THE RULES

Importantly, the Buddhist tradition introduced these five steps not as a perfect remedy for all interpersonal conflicts, but as ways to improve skillful communication. We may use them to deal with most conflicts effectively, but exceptions will always exist. When Sariputta clarified to the Buddha the effectiveness of this five-step process, the Buddha raised this important point:

> Still, Sariputta, even though you follow these methods
> of communication, some individuals may not agree
> with your suggestions.[12]

This statement reflects the Buddha's great insight that the five-step method will not solve every interpersonal conflict, and accordingly, he invites Sariputta to explain why some people are so resistant and how we should react to them.

In response, Sariputta admitted that some listeners do resist despite the speaker's skillful communication methods; and he cited the listeners' long-cultivated personality attributes as a clear reason for such resistance. The Buddha praised Sariputta and encouraged him to promote the recommended techniques for the benefit of those who are, in fact, ready to listen. Significantly, his concluding remarks in this sutta indicate that the communication methods presented by Sariputta will encourage most, if not all people, to deal with conflict peacefully.

ADDITIONAL GUIDANCE FOR SKILLFUL COMMUNICATION
This discussion has focused on Sariputta's clarification of the Buddha's instructions for improving communication skills and successfully resolving interpersonal conflict. The Buddha himself discussed further useful tips for the same purpose. The following techniques stand out.

1. REFRAIN FROM ARGUING ON SENSITIVE TOPICS
To minimize conflicts in a relationship, the Buddha suggested we refrain from arguing on sensitive topics. Such topics include speculative concepts, those views and beliefs that have no scientific evidence for support. He clearly stated that argumentation on such issues provokes confrontation rather than consensus.

The Buddha's conversation with Kassapa, an ascetic belonging to a different system of thought, highlights his position. The Buddha maintained close relationships with teachers of other religions, visiting them regularly and having friendly conversations with them. In conversation with Kassapa, the Buddha suggested they only discuss matters on which they shared similar views, and that they leave aside disagreeable topics.[13] The objective of this approach is the continued healthy relationship between the speaker and listener.

When others introduced sensitive topics, the Buddha sometimes remained silent instead of arguing on them. Silence, he

maintained, could be better than the possible negative consequences of speaking. And sometimes the Buddha did not hesitate to agree with different views. He regarded a relationship as
more important than an argument on ever-debatable and metaphysical topics.

This assertion does not mean that the Buddha refrained from
argument altogether, nor did he ask his followers never to
argue. On numerous occasions, he argued convincingly against
certain social practices, such as discrimination. The *Digha
Nikaya I*, for instance, contains some of the Buddha's most powerful arguments. They mostly present strong rational appeals
against unjust and harmful social beliefs and practices. Regarding sensitive personal beliefs and practices, however, the
Buddha maintained that argumentation is useless, and even
harmful, for relationships.

At present, religious, political, and some social beliefs and
practices belong to this category. If a husband and a wife who
practice two different religions begin to argue about religious
beliefs, the relationship will definitely suffer. Similarly, two
friends who demean each other's social practices will pave the
way for a tense and waning relationship.

For the sake of relationships, the Buddha suggested we refrain
from arguing on such topics. He indicated that while rational
argumentation may be necessary when a belief or action causes
unwholesome effects, most religious beliefs and social practices
should be beneficial. In this situation, rather than arguing
against them, the best approach is to show them respect.

2. UNDERSTAND THAT SOME ASPECTS OF BEHAVIOR ARE UNCHANGEABLE

In order to maintain healthy relationships, we may have to
accept some less likable behavior patterns of our close associates. The Buddha identified most people as having some sort of

inner weaknesses. "A person without mental ailments is difficult to find," he claimed.[14] Some of these weaknesses include the "failure to recognize, admit, or rectify their behavior."[15] Such being the nature of some individuals, our effort to correct them would only bring disappointment and frustration. The Buddha stated that some people would naturally react with anger, ill will, and aggression to a well-intended suggestion about their behavior.[16] In such a situation, the best step is to understand and accept some behavior of our associates as unalterable although ideally every individual in any relationship needs to adjust his or her behavior instead of forcing the other person to accept it. Certain individuals may exhibit some disagreeable behavior patterns that would cause no serious threat to the relationship. Accepting such behavior seems to be more realistic than trying to change it.

The Buddha noted that self-adjustment is an important characteristic of a developed person. The same adjustment also seems to reduce some unpleasant experiences in a relationship. We may find it difficult to change others according to our own wishes, but we can improve our own thoughts and actions to suit others' behavior. We may make a deliberate effort to be patient and tolerant when we encounter some forms of disagreeable—but non-threatening—behavior in our close associates.

A husband's tendency to be silent and his wife's readiness to express herself exemplify the forms of behavior that demand tolerance and acceptance. She may want him to listen and give his feedback while he wants her to express her thoughts sparingly. However, if both partners understand each other's nature, they may accept the other's behavior instead of trying to change it. Constant complaints about the other person's lack of attention or self-expression may strain a relationship. Patience, tolerance, and eventual acceptance, in contrast, will tend to reduce conflicts.

3. PROVIDE AN OPPORTUNITY FOR IMPROVEMENT

Forgiveness and trust in human potential characterize two of the most important of the Buddha's teachings. We make mistakes. Sometimes we might make serious mistakes that will affect our relationships adversely. The Buddha urged his disciples to forgive such mistakes and to give the wrongdoer an opportunity for improvement. Such an approach will contribute to the creation of stronger relationships.

This suggestion does not mean that people must forget about all the serious wrongdoings of their spouses, friends, and other closely connected people. Instead, it means that someone's past mistakes should not cause people to condemn the person as inherently evil and incapable of having healthy relationships. We may learn from our mistakes. We have the ability to improve, and we may overcome our sullied past and become better people:

> Some persons, after being indolent in the past, become vigilant and improve later. They brighten the world just as the moon does when it is released from a cloud.[17]

The Buddha showed great confidence in human power to improve. And giving others a chance to improve may be a judicious approach to solving any interpersonal conflict.

This approach may be more relevant to intimate relationships than to any others. Many who are committed to a relationship expect their partners to be faithful, but these expectations do not always come true. Violation of trust is not uncommon in our society. Some may find their partners being vulnerable to sensual pleasure. The more one loves the other, the more troubling the unexpected discovery can be. Our culture encourages us to torment the "sinners" relentlessly. However, when we allow ourselves to revel in our resentment, we inevitably force a painful end to the relationship. A more skillful approach might be to allow the other to better understand the nature of his or her wrongdoing and allow time to correct it.

The Buddha explained that attraction to the opposite gender is the most powerful natural human drive. "I have seen no other sight, sound, smell, taste, or touch than that of a woman to arrest the heart of a man," he said.[18] A woman can also be attracted to a man in the same way[19] (and we can, of course, extend this to nonheterosexual relationships as well). This situation, one's acting upon inherent urges, may be considered natural. Nevertheless, human beings have also developed a realistic way of thinking to counter their natural tendencies. Given an opportunity, they may understand the benefits of a realistic approach to their natural urges. That understanding may enable them to correct the mistakes that damage their intimate relationships.

The most important step to correct oneself and to restrengthen a relationship is to "see the mistake as it is, accept the wrong, and to determine not to repeat it."[20] When we do this, we are being the kind of person the Buddha called *pandita*, or developed persons.

4. SEEK A HARMONIOUS SEPARATION

In everything, we find exceptions. Duties and obligations, communication skills, and other techniques are meant to reduce, not to eliminate, the conflicts that might exist in a relationship. Despite a genuine effort, some may find their problems insoluble. What did the Buddha say about these unhappy and unwanted relationships? How did he want his followers to react to those who are no longer close to them?

The Buddha identified several factors that lead to the appropriate termination of a relationship: the other party's continued wrong conduct which goes on unchecked, danger arising from the relationship, or the identification of the futility of continuing it. In any of these situations, the Buddha clearly accepted individual choice as the ultimate criterion for a decision. He told his followers to retreat from an unsuitable relationship just as a king returns from a conquered land.[21]

However, this individual freedom does not support hasty, adamant, and lopsided conclusions; rather, rational and ethical evaluations should precede any final decisions. One must make sure that one's decision will benefit, rather than adversely affect, the people involved in the relationship, including oneself. Anyone has the right to stop a relationship if the decision meets these criteria.

The Buddha's advice to Upali, a follower and close companion of the Jain leader Mahavira, bears witness to this conclusion. At the request of his master, Upali visited the Buddha to defeat him in an argument. However, after listening to the Buddha, Upali found his teaching worthier than Mahavira's and wished to become the Buddha's follower. In reply, the Buddha said, "You must evaluate your decision further; it is better for a respectable person like yourself to examine and evaluate this decision."[22] After Upali assured the Buddha that his decision was well informed, the Buddha allowed him to leave Mahavira and to become a follower of the Buddha. Rationally investigated individual choice is the key factor that determined Upali's decision.

The same evaluation is applicable to a more personal relationship as well. During the Buddha's time men and women who were married left their partners and lived a secluded life in an effort to achieve self-purification. The Buddha never discouraged them so long as their self-development would cause no harm to their spouses and children. For instance, he commended Ugga, a wealthy householder, for providing for the welfare and protection of his (Ugga's) wives before leaving them.[23] Obviously, the Buddha did not mean that one could leave a husband or a wife in search of different pleasures—yet, he indicated that harmonious separation from an unwanted relationship would be better than continuing with it.

The Buddha also advised people about how they should react to their former friends and associates after a relationship had ended. His discussion with Kesi, a horse trainer, indicates that one should first leave aside hatred and revengeful thoughts toward former companions even if they have caused distress in a relationship. Kesi told the Buddha that he (Kesi) would kill the horses that would be unwilling to cooperate in training. The Buddha said in response that he should, instead, leave aside the people who would no longer be tamable or cooperative.[24]

In the Buddha's teachings, one's pursuit of hatred and revenge is never encouraged even if one has been misused or hurt by another in a relationship. The Buddha taught that one would never find inner peace as long as one clings to the misdeeds done by another person in the past.[25] Taking appropriate actions against maltreatment is always recommended—however, as the Buddha saw it, pursuit of hatred would only aggravate the agony that has already sprung from an unhappy relationship. People make their lives miserable by dwelling on broken relationships, but they may find harmony in life by learning to forgive and forget.

SUMMARY

The Buddha and his disciple Sariputta offered their community members invaluable guidance to deal peacefully with interpersonal conflicts. The improvement of communication skills and the development of skillful attitudes and behavior are required for this purpose. The Buddha emphasized that most problems arising in close relationships can be dealt with successfully through these methods. Yet, some relationships are liable to fail however hard one tries to make them work. On such occasions, separation would be the most effective way to free oneself from the burden of conflicts. One needs to regard separation not as a method of revenge, but as a step to help oneself and one's partner.

CHAPTER 9: SUCCEEDING SOCIALLY

> The Buddha cordially welcomes all kinds of
>   people.
> He is friendly, unassuming, and accessible to all....
> People of all social classes respect him.
>   Brahmin teacher Sonadanda,
>   *The Long Discourses of the Buddha*

Besides dealing with interpersonal relationships, the Buddha also guided his lay followers in right attitudes and behavior for successful social life and healthy social relationships. As thousands of people from all social groups earnestly sought membership in his new community, the Buddha strove for the most effective ways to maintain unity within it, as well as with other social groups. This chapter discusses what he recommended to make his lay followers' social lives happy and peaceful.

RIGHT ATTITUDE AND BEHAVIOR IN SEVEN STEPS

Change of attitude and behavior are among the Buddha's key points for establishing and maintaining healthy social relationships. His guidance is categorized in the following seven steps:

1. DISCARD ATTITUDES AND ACTIONS BASED ON
CASTE, RACE, AND COLOR

In order to enhance their social relationships, the Buddha persuaded people to disregard beliefs and practices based on caste, race, and color. This message indicates one of his crucial objectives, and one we have come across in previous chapters. For over forty-five years, the Buddha strove tirelessly to convince society that caste, race, and color should be immaterial. He made every effort to influence people's attitudes and behavior, expecting all social groups to live together peacefully.

To understand his voice and actions against caste, race, and color discrimination, we must first look at the marked social differences at that time. Social groupings were predominantly based on the caste of each individual. Brahmins, the architects of the caste system, asserted that they were the most respectable persons in society. Those belonging to the royal caste came second, followed by the common public and servants.

In this social structure, people maintained unhealthy attitudes and behavior. Those in the "higher castes" viewed others as inferior; consequently, their arrogance and strong sense of superiority dominated their attitude toward other social groups. Members of the "lower castes," in the meantime, developed a strong sense of inferiority. The Shudra caste, in particular, could have no other occupation than serving the members of the three higher castes. Religious practices and intercaste marriages were also prohibited to the Shudras. Obviously these thoughts, feelings, and actions did not represent correct social attitudes or behavior for healthy social relationships.

To rectify this unpleasant situation, the Buddha first encouraged society to change its attitudes—thus launching in his society an attitudinal revolution. He persuaded people to accept that every individual was equal by birth, and he asserted that

neither color nor wealth changed human equality. The following quotation conveys the Buddha's basic message:

> I do not call one a better or a worse person because of
> one's birth in a high-class family. I do not call one a
> better or a worse person because of one's color. I do
> not call one a better or a worse person because of one's
> wealth.[1]

With this important message, the Buddha presented rational
and emotional arguments to influence the rigid mentality of his
society. On the one hand, he appealed to those in the higher
class to abandon their false beliefs and wrong practices; on the
other hand, he persuaded the underprivileged class to identify
their rights and abilities.

He argued that the prevalent social attitudes and behavior
were based on social rather than absolute truths. When some
traditional groups maintained that the caste system was a divine
creation, the Buddha pointed out it was a human creation—and
that useless, baseless social truths should give way to new truths
based on rationality and humanism. "All four castes are equal in
my teaching," the Buddha said. "When the waters of four great
rivers flow into the ocean, the water is known as ocean water.
Similarly, in my society people of all castes are equal."[2]

The same assertion is applicable to racism, the inhuman practice that still exists in some societies. The Buddha did not
specifically mention race discrimination because racism was not
an issue in his society, where whatever racial differences existed
had been incorporated into the caste system. Only color discrimination, also a major component in modern racism, pre-
vailed in that culture. The Buddha's strong opposition to the
caste system and to color discrimination vindicates that he was
against racism as well.

2. PROMOTE WOMEN'S RIGHTS.

The Buddha also suggested that society needs to show respect toward women, welcome their intellectual skills, and encourage their leadership in social activities. This attitude and behavior, in turn, would enhance healthy social relationships between men and women.

The importance of this emphasis on women's rights can be evaluated in the light of related views held by the Buddha's society. Gender discrimination was at its height at the time. As in most ancient societies, female rights were suppressed. Men held the social power, and they regarded women as objects for sensual satisfaction, bearers of children, and caretakers of daily chores at home. In this social situation, the dignity and intellectual strength of women received hardly any attention.

The Buddha persuaded his society to change these attitudes and behaviors toward women. His recognition of women's intellectual strength as equal to men's clearly enabled people to change their narrow-minded attitudes toward women.

When Ananda asked the Buddha whether women had the strength to achieve the highest inner purification, the Buddha replied, "Yes, a woman is capable of achieving the highest result (arahatta phala) in the renounced life."[3] With this assertion, he allowed ordination for women. And then, similar to ordained male disciples, female disciples also achieved the highest inner purification and earned great respect from society. This positive change was an eye-opener for people who had devalued females.

The Buddha also indicated that, in order for them to live with dignity, women's own attitudes toward themselves should improve. Especially, women should identify their own skills that society had suppressed. One sutta portrays, in the voice of Mara, evil personified, the general social evaluation of women's wisdom:

If there is any higher and rare mental achievement, it can only be acquired by skillful men, not by women who naturally have narrow skills.

In reply to Mara's comments, Bhikkhuni Soma said:

You may speak your words to a person who would recognize himself or herself only by gender distinction. To a person who has developed concentration, possesses wisdom, and sees truth as it is, womanhood is no barrier at all.[4]

Her answer provides a lucid example of the attitude the Buddha wanted women to have about themselves. With great confidence in their intellectual strength, they should never allow others to devalue their skills and abilities. In brief, they should resist gender discrimination. Then their own self-esteem would enable them to live dignified lives, among themselves, as well as with men.

As social and spiritual leaders, the ordained females in the Buddha's society brought about a revolutionary change in sixth-century B.C.E. India. People flocked to their sanctuaries for spiritual and social guidance. They also proved to be the persuasive speakers in the Buddha's society as, like the ordained male disciples, they took the Buddha's message into society and convinced people that social change was necessary for social progress.

The Buddha paved the way for society to accept these various active and influential roles of women. In general, he emphasized that people must identify, promote, and respect women's intellectual strength, as well as their skills, capabilities, and active role in social and religious leadership. This improvement of attitude and behavior promoted healthy social relationships.

3. ACCEPT AND PROMOTE SOCIAL UNITY AND TOGETHERNESS

The Buddha was one of the first social reformers to advocate unity and togetherness—integration, as we may call it today—in order to create healthy social relationships. Instead of remaining within their traditional social frameworks, people were invited to mingle and work together for common goals. He strongly believed that togetherness, not separation, would enable people to leave aside social, cultural, and racial differences, and to appreciate each other.

The Buddha's establishment of a new society within a traditional, caste-dominated culture signifies his most innovative step to promote unity among diverse peoples.

He planned his society creatively. The caste-based traditional society consisted of four groups: religious leaders, warriors, common public, and servants. The Buddha also divided his society into four sections: ordained males, ordained females, laymen, and laywomen.

He assertively and unequivocally stated that people of all castes were equal in his society. An ordained person from any caste, for instance, enjoyed equal rights with all other ordained disciples. Brahmins, rulers, farmers, traders, and traditionally categorized "servants" enjoyed similar rights and maintained unity and togetherness in his new society.

Within his lifetime, the Buddha's new society emerged as the most powerful social force to challenge unjust social values, attitudes, and actions in traditional Indian society. Hundreds of thousands of people from all social groups joined in and lived peacefully, discarding the differences with which they grew up.

As people of various ethnicities and social backgrounds formed and maintained close relationships, they came to understand each other and learned to leave aside prejudices and biased attitudes. As attitudes improved, behavior toward one another also improved. All members of the Buddha's society began treating each other as human beings worthy of respect.

Thus the Buddha, through his words and deeds, introduced integration as a most innovative and effective concept to improve people's attitudes and behavior in social relationships.

4. RESPECT PEOPLE FOR THEIR INNER VALUES AND UPRIGHT CONDUCT

Having rejected all forms of discrimination based on caste, race, color, and sex, the Buddha persuaded society to respect people for their inner values and upright conduct. This improved attitude is crucial for people to enjoy a successful social life. The following statement summarizes the Buddha's key attitude:

> One does not become a respectable person by
> birth.
> One does not become a disgraceful person by
> birth, either.
> One becomes a respectable person by action;
> One becomes a disgraceful person by action.[5]

"Birth" here means caste, race, color, sex, and so on. After rejecting such irrational criteria, the Buddha identified individual action (kamma) as the most important criterion for gaining appreciation or disrespect. "Action" denotes intention-oriented words, deeds, and thoughts. A person whose actions are motivated by wholesome intention deserves respect. Those who act with unwholesome intention are liable to disgrace.

Immediately after discarding any evaluation based on caste, race, and color, the Buddha clarified his position further:

> If someone from any family refrains from destroying life,
> from taking what is not given [e.g., stealing, corruption],
> from enjoying sensual pleasure in the wrong way, from
> lying, from speaking filthy, abusive, and harmful lan-
> guage, and from entertaining greedy, malevolent, and
> misleading views, that person I call better than others.[6]

The phrase "someone from any family" is broad in meaning.
"Someone" can be a man or a woman, of any age, and living in
any part of the world. "Any family" rules out the importance of
caste, race, creed, color, and wealth as criteria for accepting or
rejecting people. The Buddha instructed society to reject such
fragile measurements and to respect people for their wholesome conduct and noble thoughts. Absence of "greedy, malev-
olent, and misleading views" signifies inner development; other
stated actions indicate the development of external behavior. A
sound combination of outer adjustment and inner development
is required to gain respect.

On the other hand, this assertion does not mean that society
should condemn those who are not in accord with established
social norms. The Buddha pointed out that our social duties
include the readiness to help people understand and follow
those values that are meaningful, both to themselves and to
society. We must always try to understand people, show compassion toward them, and be ready to help them. When it
comes to appreciation and respect, however, we may value a
person who has a developed character.

In this way, the Buddha encouraged us to respect people
based on their upright conduct and inner development, rather
than caste, race, color, gender, or wealth. This improved attitude makes social relationships stable and meaningful.

5. APPRECIATE PEOPLE'S SKILLS AND ABILITIES
WITHOUT DISCRIMINATION

The Buddha encouraged appreciation of people's skills and abilities as another way to enhance individual attitudes and behavior in social life. Through his words and deeds, he emphasized that these skills should be rewarded, and that caste, race, color, personal connections, or any other irrational criterion should never influence our appreciation of people's skills and abilities.

The appointment of Sariputta and Moggallana as the Buddha's two chief disciples demonstrates his admiration based on skills. Moggallana, who belonged to the working class before becoming a bhikkhu, was dark in complexion while Sariputta was fair. But their complexions were never an issue for the Buddha. He appointed them as his chief disciples because he knew that they were the most capable persons for those positions.

The Buddha's selection of Upali as head of all disciplinary actions in this new widespread society reaffirms his steadfast position in this regard. Upali was the barber who served the princes in the Buddha's clan. When the princes followed in the Buddha's footsteps and became ordained disciples, Upali also wished to enter the Order. Not only did the Buddha readily grant Upali's request, he also guided Upali's spiritual progress. As time passed, Upali emerged as one of the most knowledgeable, skillful, and well-disciplined monks. Thus when the Buddha offered titles to his ordained disciples, Upali became the head of all disciplinary action.

By assigning this prestigious position to Upali, the Buddha provided a solid example for his community. He encouraged his followers to refrain from discrimination and to grant people their due positions. Interestingly, the Buddha allowed the former barber Upali to supervise the discipline of nobles, princes, and the Buddha's own ordained relatives.

One of the Buddha's female disciples, Kajangala, is another example of how the Buddha persuaded society to appreciate people for their knowledge and skill. In his male-dominated society, the Buddha stood well ahead of its social values. The following episode and related teaching is a unique and apt example of how society was persuaded to admire the abilities of women, without falling victim to gender-bias:

When Kajangala went to a remote area to convey the Buddha's teaching, people gathered at her hermitage to listen to her. Kajangala's teaching impressed the visitors, but they were not fully satisfied because of their partiality to male dominance. Eventually, they decided to visit the Buddha to clear up their doubts. Walking a long distance, they met with him and explained what his female disciple had taught—and wondered whether a female was wise enough to teach them. The Buddha replied:

> Her answer is excellent! That is excellent, household-ers. Kajangala is a wise woman. If you were to come to me and ask about the meaning of this, I would give just the same explanation as that given by Kajangala. Indeed, what you heard from her is the right answer, and so should you bear it in mind.[7]

Gender was never a barrier for the Buddha's appreciation of knowledge, skills, and abilities. And he urged us to cleanse our own minds of gender bias. Significantly, he praised Kajangala's wisdom and skill so greatly that he identified her skill as similar to his own.

Overall, the Buddha guided society to appreciate people's knowledge, skills, and abilities without discrimination. Improving their attitudes and developing values beyond traditional and social truths that have no rational basis would clearly facilitate social relationships.

6. LOOK AT DIVERSE THEORIES, VIEWS, AND PRACTICES WITH PATIENCE, TOLERANCE, AND OPEN-MINDEDNESS

In his endeavor to promote healthy social relationships, the Buddha advocated patience, tolerance, and open-mindedness toward different theories and practices. As he suggested, we need to open our minds to what others say, think, believe, and practice instead of becoming mired in a rigid belief system.

On the one hand, the scientific outlook of the Buddha's teaching encouraged him to show openness to new theories. In his philosophy, no "-isms" existed: he refused to promote any speculative concepts to support people's decisions. The Buddha's conversation with Vaccha, a visitor to his monastery, confirms his position:

> The Buddha: I have seen the adverse effects of taking speculative views as truths, so I am not attached to any of the speculations [that you have just mentioned].
> Vaccha: Still, do you have any speculative views of your own?
> The Buddha: Speculative views of my own? Vaccha, I have broken free of clinging to any speculations.[8]

The Pali term the Buddha used to mean "speculative concepts" is *ditthi* together with *gata*. Any view or belief that has no evidence is a *ditthi; gata* means "taken as true." When one internalizes a speculative belief as absolute truth, one is identified as *ditthigata*.

The Buddha had freed himself from any clinging to speculative concepts, and he encouraged all his followers to do the same. This basic principle offered his followers the freedom to examine and evaluate various theories, beliefs, and practices in terms of humanistic and pragmatic values.

On the other hand, the Buddha's acceptance of some alleged absolute truths as social truths further persuades society to show openness to views, beliefs, and practices. From his viewpoint, most "truths" are social constructions. The *Agganna Sutta* asserts, for instance, that law, kingship, and religion are all social truths created for the benefit of humankind, in an effort to organize and regulate society.[9]

Unorganized ancient society so badly needed a ruler that people jointly selected a leader who was originally known as Maha Sammata, or the Great Elect. Religion came into existence as some people, disappointed with the evil deeds of the common public, started their spiritual development.[10] In brief, the Buddha clearly asserted that society created truths for pragmatic reasons.

Based on these assertions, the Buddha did not oppose the alteration, replacement, or modification of those truths if the proposed changes would be more humanistic and beneficial. As he pointed out, those who irrationally resist such changes have taken their own concepts as absolute, unalterable, or non-replaceable truths. They belligerently claim, "Only this is the truth; all others are false," without being open to other truths.[11]

The concept of living together, for instance, would appear to someone as wrong because he or she has embraced the concept of marriage as the only truth for a male and a female to start their family life. In the teaching of the Buddha, we do not find such absolute truths and ideals. Therefore, the novelty, difference, or changeability of any idea is accepted on humanistic and pragmatic grounds.

In general, the Buddha advocated a patient, tolerant, and open-minded approach to different theories, views, and practices. Such an approach enables us to minimize social conflicts and enhance our social relationships.

7. ACCEPT ARGUMENT NOT AS A WEAPON, BUT AS A QUEST FOR TRUTH

In the previous chapter, we discussed the Buddha's view that those in personal relationships need to refrain from arguing on sensitive issues. The same rule is applicable to our social relationships as well. "Those who are trapped in speculative concepts argue that their views are true," the Buddha taught. "However, when others refute these concepts in a gathering, anger, shame, and suffering will arise."[12] We find no benefits in using argument as a means to demolish the opposition.

Further elaborating on his position, the Buddha went on to say, "Whatever speech I know to be factually true, connected with the goal, but not liked by others and disagreeable to them, I do not utter."[13] Our social relationships may run smoothly when we refrain from challenging others' personal views, beliefs, and practices.

Nevertheless, as the previous chapter discussed, the Buddha never encouraged us to refrain from arguing altogether. Particularly in our social life, we need to accept and practice argumentation as an effort to search for truth, not as a weapon to attack others. Especially, we need to argue using facts, evidence, and rational claims and reasons, not using mere assumptions and speculations. Also, we need to respect the convincing arguments of others.

The following teaching sheds light on this important advice. While explaining his reluctance to argue on the concept of human existence in past and future lives, the Buddha said:

> When someone asks me a question about future life, I may ask the person another question about future life. When the questioner [tries to] please me with an answer, I may [try to] please the questioner with an answer [of my own]. Therefore let us leave aside the

questions related to past existence. Let us leave aside the questions related to future existence. I will tell you [what I understand as] the truth. When the cause exists, the effect comes into existence. From the arising of the cause, the effect arises. When the cause does not exist, the effect does not come to be. When the cause ceases, the effect will cease.[14]

The validity of this explanation depends on two factors. First, our own opposition to others' speculative concepts would hardly lead to an agreement; therefore, such talk is meaningless. Second, an agreeable conclusion can be arrived at only by discussing the issues that have proof. The last three lines of this quotation contain the formula of causal argument that the Buddha constantly employed to strengthen his claims.

Obviously, usefulness was the main criterion for selecting some topics for argumentation. The following passage shows how and why the Buddha would argue on selected topics:

Some recluses and Brahmins are skillful, subtle, experienced in argumentation, and hair-splitters.... At some points, they and I agree, and, at some other points, we do not. Some of the things they approve, we also approve. Some of the points they disapprove, we also disapprove.... Therefore let us leave aside those things we do not agree with [things we do not want to talk about]. As to those we agree with, let the wise ask questions about them, ask for reasons concerning them, and talk them over.[15]

This shows us the attitude the Buddha maintained regarding controversial issues in society. From this we can learn that we do not always have to conform to all social truths or simply accept certain views and actions that would appear to be unsound and unfair. Both parties, for the sake of the best possible solution to a problem or answer to a question, should be willing to accept the soundness of the opposite argument.

SUMMARY

The Buddha strove to instill and improve attitudes and behavior in his followers' social relationships. With his humanistic and rationalistic approach, he persuaded them to abandon class, creed, race, color, gender, and wealth as criteria for evaluating others. He urged them to respect people for their uprightness, skills, and other qualifications; and he encouraged his listeners to impartially examine various views, theories, and practices. While he preferred not to argue on highly sensitive and controversial speculations, the Buddha was well prepared for any argument—as a truth-searching effort, rather than a medium for confrontation.

CHAPTER 10: THE BUDDHA'S VIEW ON DECISION-MAKING

I have seen no other cause than the presence of false views to block the origination of right thoughts in the mind and to corrupt the right thoughts already present in the mind. I have seen no other cause than the presence of correct view to inspire right thoughts in the mind and to improve the right thoughts already present in the mind.

The Buddha, *The Numerical Discourses*

Decision-making is widely discussed in the Buddha's teachings to his lay disciples. He spoke consistently about the pitfalls of poor decision-making and offered well-formulated principles for making wiser decisions. As a prerequisite for making rational decisions, he also taught the elimination of false reasoning—the removal of inner viruses, so to speak.

DIVERSE VIEWS ON DECISION-MAKING

Before we look at the Buddha's view on decision-making, we must first consider the diverse views of his contemporaries. On the one hand, there were the traditionalists who denied the individual's right to make decisions. They claimed that decisions for the people had already been made by tradition, divine power, religious texts, and the gurus who had cultivated super-natural powers; and society had to accept those decisions as undeniable truths, accordingly.

For example, members of the royal caste were to be rulers and warriors, never teachers of sacred texts. Divine power and tradition had allegedly assigned these duties to the royal caste and they were never to be challenged. According to this traditionalist view, individuals had no choice but to follow the decisions that had been made for them.

Materialists, on the other hand, rejected traditional views. They asserted that individual self-interest should be the basis of decision-making. If a decision leads to one's own happiness, they argued, one should not hesitate to make that decision—regardless of its negative consequences for others. They urged people to borrow money and enjoy life; since death is the ultimate end, self-satisfaction should be life's primary goal. And they used logic and speculative theories to support their view of individual self-interest as the basis for decision-making.

The Buddha rejected both the traditionalist's denial of individual rights and the materialist's overemphasis on self-interest as criteria for making decisions. Instead he introduced new principles for decision-making, including rationality (broad reasoning), humanism (presence of wholesome thoughts), and pragmatism (practical usefulness).

Although he clearly welcomed the individual's right and freedom to make decisions, the Buddha asserted that these rights and freedom must be used correctly. What's more, the Buddha taught that prior to making any decision, one should make sure one harbors no fallacies to interfere with one's judgment.

FALSE REASONING, WRONG DECISIONS

The word *moha* (illusion) actually suggests, in the broader sense, the presence of fallacious argument in reasoning. This error

clouds the mind, hides the truth, and makes the decision irrational and unwise. In order to judge wisely, we must first be
aware that *moha* presents a threat to right decision-making.

Several suttas—the *Kalama, Bhaddiya, Canki,* and others—present ten kinds of fallacies in reasoning.

FALLACY 1: REPORTED INFORMATION IS TRUE

The Buddha observed that one fallacy that may affect our ability to make right decisions is the automatic acceptance of any
reported information as true. This seems to include our readiness to accept rumor, hearsay, reports, or any information coming from sources other than our own direct experience.

Importantly, this statement does not mean that we should
reject all reports and secondhand information in order to make
rational decisions. Rather, it means we should respond to such
information cautiously and with an open mind. As the Buddha
explained: "What is convincingly reported may be empty, void,
[and] false while what is not reported would [actually] be fact
and the truth."[1] In other words, reported information may cause
"twofold results," a phrase that indicates a report to be either
true or false.[2] Therefore, "an intelligent person should reflect"
upon the possibility that the information coming from reports
can go either way.[3]

Thus, the Buddha urged caution when responding to any form
of secondhand information. A cautious reaction, he taught,
would clearly enhance our ability to make judicious decisions.

FALLACY 2: TRADITIONAL VALUES, BELIEFS, AND PRACTICES
ARE ACTUAL TRUTHS

The Buddha pointed out that the acceptance of tradition as
truth and the consequent submission to traditional authority
would further weaken our ability to make rational decisions. As
previously mentioned, he clearly stated in the *Agganna Sutta* that

traditional truths are in fact social and historical creations. Our dependence on these traditional truths while making decisions would mean the denial of human rationality, the basic requirement for prudent decisions.

One of the decisions based on this fallacy, the Buddha observed, was the repeated recital of hymns to please various deities. Simply because past generations had chanted these hymns, this generation did the same, without any verification of the existence of such deities. "When a string of blind men are clinging one to the other, neither can the foremost see, nor can the middle one see, nor can the hindmost see."[4] Similarly, those who blindly followed the tradition would go around in the same circle of traditional truth, failing to see its futility.

Importantly, however, this assertion does not mean that the Buddha persuaded his listeners to discard tradition altogether in order to be able to decide wisely. For instance, he remarked that parents expect their children to follow some family traditions, and children should respect that expectation.[5] Some traditional beliefs and practices, however, would require a rational evaluation before we depend on them to make important decisions. The basic lesson is that traditional authority is not an absolute truth within which we must confine ourselves while making decisions.

FALLACY 3: SOCIAL TRUTHS ARE ACTUAL TRUTHS

During the Buddha's time, social authority, in addition to traditional authority, also provided a strong reason for some social groups to justify their claims. Although connected, social authority differs from traditional authority. Advocates of social authority claimed that something would be right or wrong because society in general accepted it as such. They cited social authority in various terms such as "because they say so," "because that is the truth," and "because that is how it should be."

The young Brahmin Vasettha revealed, in conversation with

the Buddha, one such predominant social truth in the Buddha's society. Vasettha had become a follower of the Buddha, but his fellow Brahmins would not tolerate Vasettha's transformation. They criticized him, saying, "Such a course is not acceptable; it is not proper."[6] They further remarked that a Brahmin, who belonged to the so-called highest social class, should not learn under the guidance of the Buddha, a member of the ruling class.[7]

In this example, the truth held by some Brahmins—that a Brahmin should not study under a ruler—is a social truth, or a belief commonly held by a social group or the entire society. Of course, these truths were empowered by tradition, but social acceptance was the underlying reason to support these claims.

The Buddha identified dependence on social authority as a crucial obstacle to wise decisions. Referring to Vasettha's remarks, he noted that an evaluation of the historical development of the Brahmin view would confirm its falsity. He instructed his community to reject social authority, which is "just a sound of the world," as termed by the Buddha's disciple Kacchana.[8] The Pali term *ma itikiraya*—*ma*, "do not accept or take"; and *itikiraya*, "[because] thus it is said or accepted, as true"—means that social acceptance or rejection is not a dependable reason for accepting or rejecting something.

And yet, often social truths seem to be actual truths even though they are not. Social truths are so powerful that, unless we are mindful of their strength, they quickly invade our minds and overpower us. The Buddha advised us not to fall prey to irrational social truths in order to retain our ability to make correct decisions.

FALLACY 4: THE TEXTS ARE TRUE

Submission to textual authority is another pitfall that the Buddha identified as an obstruction to our rational decisions. The Vedic tradition during the Buddha's time consistently used textual authority to strengthen such beliefs as divine creation of a caste system and divine assignment of duties to each caste. Advocates of the Vedic tradition argued that society should accept these concepts as absolute truths simply because they were accepted in sacred texts. The Buddha strongly challenged this argument. He asserted that a decision based on textual authority would fail to support the decision-maker's wisdom.

The Buddha stated that the so-called sacred texts were a human creation. This statement makes the Buddha perhaps the first thinker to claim that religious truths are social constructions. As he explained, after ancient Brahmins began their religious practices, they started preparing texts.[9] Therefore, the so-called absolute truths presented in those texts could be erroneous. The decisions based on such texts could also be wrong.

Societies still tend to use texts, particularly religious texts, as a dependable criterion for decision-making. Consequently, people may arrive at conclusions that are dubious and devoid of rationality. Abortion, homosexuality, and same-sex marriage are some of the popular topics regarding which textual authority comes to the forefront.

To the Buddha, texts were never a reason to justify a claim since a decision based on mere textual authority would not reflect the decision-maker's wisdom. Rejection of textual authority, accordingly, is a clear sign of arriving at wise conclusions.

FALLACY 5: LOGICAL REASONING IS ALWAYS CORRECT

The Buddha used the word *takka* for the kind of logical reasoning he wanted his followers to be cautious about. *Trick*, the English cognate of this word, is derived from this root—and that word tells it all. Dependence on some kinds of logical reasoning can mislead the thinker. In modern argumentation, most of these tricks, or flimsy forms of reasoning, are identified as logical fallacies.

Dependence on enticing but shallow logical analogies is one form of logical reasoning that the Buddha identified as obstructive to clear thinking. During the Buddha's time, certain thinkers used such analogies to support their views. The following comparison given by Makkhali Gosala, a famous thinker of the time, is an apt example:

> When one flings a bundle of string while standing on the top of a mountain and keeps hold of one end of the string, the spool goes down to its end and then stops. Similarly, every person will continue to be born in a certain number of lives after death, and then his or her existence will cease.[10]

Even though at first blush this statement seems to be constructed logically, a closer observation demonstrates that the comparison is senseless and empty. Basically, we find no connection between a bundle of string, which is a visual object, and rebirth, a metaphysical concept. In fact, the comparison is a trick to strengthen the claim that an individual continues to be reborn a certain number of times. We fail to decide wisely if we take this logical comparison for granted.

The following conclusions exemplify several other kinds of logical reasoning that the Buddha recognized as obstructions to rational thinking:

- These ascetics are well disciplined. They have achieved enlightenment.[11]
- His ancestors from both mother's and father's sides have been Brahmins. Therefore, he is a noble person.[12]
- If the Buddha performs a miracle, the Buddha can prove his status as an enlightened person.[13]

In the first example, the Buddha remarked that the reason is an inadequate support for the claim. One would have to examine the ascetics more closely to find out whether or not they were enlightened.

In the second argument, the given reason is irrelevant because the Buddha finds no relationship between one's having Brahmin ancestors and being a noble person.

The reason in the third argument is totally unrelated to the claim. The Buddha sees no connection between one's achievement of enlightenment and one's ability to perform miracles. Adherence to these logical fallacies clearly hinders one's rational judgment.

Still, this warning does not, of course, mean that the Buddha urged society to reject logical reasoning altogether. His advice was just to be cautious. And on various occasions, he used logical argument to strengthen his claims and to counter the opposition. Nevertheless, he made it clear that total dependence on logic may prevent one from arriving at rational conclusions:

> One who uses logic may argue correctly or incorrectly; the argument may be so or otherwise. Therefore, a wise person should reflect thus: "This person uses logic to investigate. Logic may be correct or incorrect; it could be so or otherwise."[14]

What the Buddha emphasized throughout his speeches was that experience and understanding, not logical assumptions, would provide the key to wisdom. We need to evaluate logical assumptions cautiously and give priority to our own experience and wisdom in order to decide the rightness or wrongness of any action.

FALLACY 6: REASONING BASED ON IMAGINATION
AND SPECULATION IS CORRECT

The acceptance of reasoning originating in imagination and speculation can lead us to unwise decisions. The following view was held by the Brahmin tradition in the Buddha's time. It is a prime example of this error: A member of the Shudra caste must serve the other castes because Brahma created the first Shudra from Brahma's feet. The conclusion that Shudras should be servants is based solely on the imagined and speculated theory that the first Shudra was born from the creator's feet. In this argument, a Shudra is low in status because Brahma's foot is an unsuitable source for a human being. The Buddha stated that acceptance of this claim is not a wise judgment, because the reason given in favor of it is merely speculative.

The words "imagination" and "speculation" seem to need more attention in this discussion. Basically, we find two kinds of theories in society: one based on reasoning and knowledge and the other on imagination and speculation. For instance, the Theory of Evolution is said to depend on knowledge and reasoning while the Theory of Creation is based on imagination and speculation, or, alternatively, on textual authority. While the Buddha did not want his lay community members to cling to any kind of theory, he specifically persuaded them not to depend on speculative and imaginary theories for decision-making.

Still, the Buddha encouraged his society to respect rational theories for decisions. In the *Aggañña Sutta*,[15] he considered the social differences between people and concluded that social evolution could be the reason for such differences. As he noted in the same sutta, the caste system was a social creation. He then used the concept of social evolution to conclude that people of all castes should have equal rights.

The Buddha regarded rational theory to be important in decision-making. Despite his cautious approach to all theories, the Buddha respected the rationality behind a theory as a means to facilitate a wise decision. At the same time, he strongly opposed submission to speculative theories when making decisions.

As the Buddha phrased it, speculative theories are "hammered out by one's own line of thought."[16] Conceived through mere brainstorming, such theories follow their inventors' speculative skill, not true knowledge. Thus, decisions based on imagination and speculation fail to demonstrate our prudence.

FALLACY 7: HYPOTHESIZED REASONING IS CORRECT

Dependence on hypothesized reasoning, according to the Buddha's observation, is another barrier to wise decisions. Those who depend on this sort of reasoning find quick and easy answers to complex problems. However, these answers and solutions are often unrealistic, impractical, and devoid of rationality so that a decision based on hypothesized reasoning reflects little wisdom.

The following argument presented by some people in the Buddha's society exemplifies hypothesized reasoning:

> Those who belong to a lower social class by birth are incapable of achieving the mental development necessary for holy life. Therefore, people of the low classes should not be allowed to enter holy life.[17]

Highlighting the weakness of this argument, the Buddha asked, "On what strength and authority do they speak thus?"[18] In other words, the statement that people in some social groups are inherently incapable of achieving mental development has never been tested or proved. The so-called pundits, resting comfortably in plush chairs, may indulge in this type of reasoning, but it is far from the truth.

Through his own actions, the Buddha demonstrated that a decision based on this fallacious reasoning is devoid of rational thought. For instance, he ordained many people belonging to lower social classes, and helped them achieve success in their spiritual lives. By doing so, he disclaimed the view that only people of higher classes could achieve progress in spiritual life and become successful social campaigners.

Traditionalists in the Buddha's society used the word *parisuddha* (purification) to mean spiritual progress. Referring to this word, the Buddha remarked that, similar to a person in a higher class, any individual could step into a bath with soap and a scrub brush to "purify" himself or herself. The Buddha thus refused to accept hypothesized reasoning as a criterion for decisions.

His rejection of hypothesized reasoning, on the other hand, does not suggest that hypotheses are useless for rational decisions. Of course, we often hypothesize as a preparation for making decisions, but even a seemingly valid hypothesis can turn into utter falsehood when we continue to examine it. The Buddha's advice is that we need to examine our hypotheses closely in order to determine their soundness.

FALLACY 8: ONE SHOULD ACCEPT A VIEW BECAUSE IT IS COMPATIBLE WITH ONE'S OWN WAY OF THINKING

The Buddha identified the "because I like/don't like it" approach as a hindrance to wise judgment. People exhibit a tendency to embrace views simply because these views correspond with their own way of thinking. Such an approach, according to the Buddha, fails to reflect the wisdom of the decision-maker.

The reaction of the ascetic Keniya after he listened to the Buddha is a relevant example of how this fallacy may prevent one from making rational decisions.[19]

Keniya visited the Buddha to learn the Dhamma, and the text indicates that the Buddha gave an enlightening talk to his visitor. In honor of that speech, Keniya invited the Buddha and his disciples to visit his residence for a meal. Nevertheless, Keniya failed to accept the Buddha's reasoning because he (Keniya) was "pleased enough to believe what he heard from Brahmin teachers."[20] In other words, Keniya indicated that he did not want to reject what he liked even though the Buddha's counterargument exposed the irrationality in Keniya's inclination.

Notably, this fallacy constantly leads an individual toward wrong decisions in daily life. Most judgments based on mere individual preference fall into this fallacy. Those who use this fallacious reasoning may support their claims with the following reasons:

- Because I like/don't like/hate it
- Because I want/don't want it
- Because I think/don't think so

Of course, emphasis on the individual freedom to make decisions is a distinguishing characteristic in the Buddha's teaching, but mere individual preference is not. In other words, the Buddha asserted that, in addition to considering our own strong inclination toward a certain decision, we also need to evaluate other reasons. The next chapter will discuss this topic in detail, but briefly, mere individual choice failed to win the Buddha's appreciation as a wise criterion for decisions.

Upon further examination, we find that individual fondness for a certain decision connects to naturalism while readiness for further evaluation of the possible consequences of the same decision relates to rationality. Nature has given human beings a powerful urge for certain actions. Yet, putting such an urge into action without evaluating its possible effects can cause huge damage. The "because I like it" approach to justify an action touches the natural instinct of the human being, a tendency that ignores the repercussions of a particular action. This point further highlights the danger of a decision that is merely motivated by the individual's inner propensity.

As the Buddha pointed out repeatedly, desire for sensory satisfaction naturally predominates over all human behavior. In this situation, people may find many attractive views, ideas, and practices that are compatible with their way of thinking. However, the Buddha made it clear that submission to such natural urges would not bear witness to the decision-maker's wisdom. A wise person would be patient enough to evaluate other reasons rather than surrender to his or her own inner tendency.

FALLACY 9: ONE'S PERSUASIVE SKILL VALIDATES THE MESSAGE

This fallacy means that a person who is capable of presenting an idea skillfully is also presenting a right idea. The Buddha encouraged his listeners to reject this criterion. He taught that we should not allow other people's persuasive skill or rhetorical authority to dominate our conclusions.

In his society, the Buddha found many people striving to influence the decisions of an enthusiastic audience. These persuaders, who argued on various topics related to religious, social, and spiritual matters, used their argumentative power and rhetorical skill to influence people. They spoke fluently, defeated opponents, and appealed to the audience in a convincing way. Some of them were very famous, and victorious in most of their debates with opponents. Saccaka, for instance, boasted, "Even a lifeless wooden post would tremble and shake when I challenge it with my words; so why should a human being not!"[21]

The phrase "persuasive skill" includes not only the speaker's argumentative skill, but also his or her rhetorical tactics. To make rational decisions, one should not become a victim of these tactics. The Buddha was very much aware of such techniques when he recognized right timing and right understanding of the audience as requirements for persuasion. Skillful persuaders—or manipulators, as they are often best termed—may select the most appropriate time to dupe us into making unwise decisions. The Buddha reminded us to be mindful of these tactics.

This statement, however, does not mean that rhetorical strength always fails to lead people to right decisions. The Buddha emphatically stated that rational argumentation always leads to right conclusions. His concern relates, instead, to manipulation by skillful persuaders who used various rhetorical techniques to present themselves as the most capable people to lead society into making right decisions. These apparently capable but actually deceptive individuals strengthen their claims by way of rhetorical skill—and the listener should always be mindful that rhetorical skill alone will not lead to wise decisions.

FALLACY 10: INDIVIDUAL AUTHORITY IS A DEPENDABLE CRITERION FOR MAKING DECISIONS

The Buddha also maintained that submission to individual authority could obstruct our ability to make wise decisions. This fallacy and the one above are closely linked, but they differ in the following way. While rhetorical authority focuses on one's ability to manipulate the listener through rhetoric, individual authority emphasizes the power behind one's personality. Society may tend to accept the views and respect the guidance of those who have or seem to have strong personalities. According to the Buddha, however, this social attitude is not necessarily correct.

Many components combine to enhance the power of personality in different individuals. Characteristics, knowledge, social status, experience, skill, appearance, and apparent qualifications play a major role in constructing a strong personality. Such a personality seems to have magical power: it possesses enormous ability to influence. The Buddha noticed the danger lurking behind individual authority. He observed the possibility that those who truly possessed a powerful personality, as well as those who professed to possess it, might lead society to arrive at the wrong conclusions.

The following examples show how influential people in the Buddha's society displayed personal authority to influence others:

- Brahma revealed to me that the caste system is a divine creation. Therefore, you should not challenge the caste system.
- After developing the mind through strenuous effort, I realized that karma is unchangeable. Therefore, you have to accept your destiny.
- He is a student of a distinguished teacher. He has acquired all the knowledge required to be a teacher. So he is capable of teaching you the right practice.

The assumed strength in each of these examples is individual authority: divine favor in the first, self-realization in the second, and social status and self-fulfillment in the third.

The authority expressed in the first two examples is questionable: nobody knows or can test whether the asserted authority is true. In the third example, the authority may be true or can at least be checked. Overall, the claims in all the given sentences depend on individual authority, either pretended or actual.

The Buddha warned that we would find no way to ascertain that the self-proclaimed authority in the first two examples is genuine. And even though the authority given in the third example might be true, it does not guarantee the speaker's ability or genuine intention to lead the listener along the right path. Therefore, to decide wisely, the listener should first make the following inquiries:

- Is the alleged authority real?
- If it is real, does the authority justify the person's ability?
- Is the authoritative person sincere in his or her motives?

In a remarkable statement, the Buddha asked Upali—a businessman who was willing to accept the Buddha as his new spiritual leader—to make a deeper inquiry into the Buddha and his teaching.[22] Such an inquiry would enable Upali to select his leader wisely. Confidence in a person who falsely claims to have qualifications and abilities may lead us to make irrational decisions.

Importantly, the Buddha's advice does not suggest that the ideas of an authoritative person should be rejected. In several teachings, he stressed that one should rely on personal authority only after a thorough investigation. In many of his teachings, he advised turning to authoritative people in a particular field, instead of making our own uninformed decisions. But one should first be convinced that the alleged authority is true, and that the authoritative person possesses the ability and intention to guide one along the right path.

COMBINATIONS OF FALSE REASONING—AND BEYOND

The Buddha also noticed that some of his contemporaries used various fallacious reasoning methods to heighten their claims. For example, some traditionalists used reports, individual authority, logic, and snap reasoning to amplify the claim that they were superior to other social classes. In his conversation with Bharadvaja, a young Brahmin who was interested in the

Buddha's teaching, the Buddha took each of these fallacies for analysis, saying, "First, you cited individual authority, and now you are talking about the authority of the report."[23] The Buddha examined each of these fallacies to show how misleading they could be. Then, he concluded:

> For a wise person who strives to discover and preserve the truth, this [the use of fallacious reasoning] is not sufficient to decide that something is the truth, and others are false.[24]

We observe that some social groups at present extensively use a combination of false reasoning methods to add more power to their claims, and, of course, they succeed occasionally. The claim that people should fight for the sake of religion is an example in this regard. Textual, traditional, and social authorities would be the reasons in favor of this claim.

Just one kind of drug impairs a sober individual, but a cocktail has devastating effects. Similarly, a single form of false reasoning may affect a person's wise judgment, but a combination, if accepted unquestioningly, would hypnotize the person and paralyze his or her mind. We use the word "brainwashed" to identify the mental status of a person who has fallen prey to various forms of false reasoning. This mental degeneration, the ultimate outcome of one's total surrender to several forms of authority, can amount to refusal to make independent decisions—let alone wise ones!

AWAKENING TO TRUTH

When the Buddha explained to Bharadvaja that false reasoning leads an individual toward wrong decisions, the latter made the following request:

To what extent, sir, does one see the truth?
What awakens one to the truth? We are asking
the Buddha about awakening to the truth.[25]

The detailed answer to this question should stand as timeless guidance for relieving individuals of the burden of false reasoning. Those who preserved this sutta seem to have reorganized its content, but the basic steps to balanced reasoning remain intact.

In this teaching, the Buddha first identified self-imposed imprisonment within one's own mental world as the worst hindrance to liberation from false reasoning.

He then introduced several useful steps toward inner freedom. Having a desire for learning, striving for the truth, listening, approaching, testing what is learned, and weighing the different views and practices are some of the interrelated steps that can help one eliminate false reasoning. To clarify their effectiveness, these suggestions deserve more attention.

The Buddha always recognized the human capacity for self-improvement, and one's ability to eliminate false reasoning is part of that. However, if a person tends to close his or her mind only to take refuge in the fallacies embodied within it, he or she would find no way to escape. Essentially, interest and readiness are the most important prerequisites to the freedom of thought. The Buddha noted that desire within the individual would serve as a forerunner to effort, the next step for advancement. Contrary to some people's opinions, the Buddha actually taught about individual need and inner desire:

Need provides great help for effort. If need does not originate within, one will not make an effort. If desire does originate within, one will make an effort. Therefore, desire is extremely helpful for effort [to find the truth].[26]

The Buddha persuaded us to show an interest in the wide world of ideas, views, and practices as a preparation for the elimination of false reasoning. Once the seed of interest germinates and sprouts inside, the mind will naturally search, investigate, compare, and contrast—and eventually select wise criteria for decisions. As the Buddha observed, searching, approaching, listening, testing, and weighing the different truths pave the way for interested individuals to select advanced criteria for decision-making.

The Buddha's message to those who entertain various fallacies is an optimistic one: he believed that individuals possess the potential to emerge from fallacious argumentation. Openness permits the influx of different views and is a welcome way to realize this potential. As our horizons broaden, we discover better and more profound reasons to defend or refute a multitude of thoughts and actions.

SUMMARY

The Buddha identified fallacious reasoning as a formidable threat to rational thinking. Blinded by numerous fallacies, most people fail to show wise judgment in their decision-making. The Buddha recognized ten fallacies that constantly spring up in our minds to thwart the wisdom of our decisions. While each may work alone, fallacies sometimes combine to disturb our judgment yet further. Openness to diverse views and ideas is an effective step toward freedom from false reasoning. Fallacies lose their firm grip on our minds as we continue to examine the wide world of ideas—and elimination of fallacious reasoning is the gateway to wise decisions.

CHAPTER 11: CORRECT REASONING, RIGHT DECISIONS

> If you understand that this action is right,
> harmless, blissful, beneficial, and admirable,
> take that action and follow it.
> The Buddha, *The Numerical Discourses*

Elimination of fallacious reasoning is just the beginning of rational decision-making. The Buddha stated that we must then begin the process of arriving at the most appropriate decision. To understand that process, let us first look into the mental status of the individual who has bid farewell to various forms of false reasoning. We will then see what the Buddha considered to be the correct, or true, process of evaluation leading toward correct decisions.

Importantly, by helping us to eliminate false reasoning, the Buddha helped us to secure what is needed for right decisions: inner freedom. We have seen how the various forms of fallacious argumentation restrict our mental capacity and disturb our reasoning power, and how, when these no longer interfere with our decision-making, we find no limitations on our rational thinking and our freedom of thought.

We need to exercise extreme caution, however, while discussing the concept of inner freedom. The absence of fallacious reasoning does not, according to the Buddha, mean we have the right to do anything we want. Instead, by helping to eliminate false reasons, the Buddha paved the way for us to travel beyond social, cultural, religious, and intellectual restrictions. He urged us to examine the other reasons for our decisions and to *know* why we should make, or refrain from making, certain decisions. "Know" is the key word. The Buddha offered us unrestricted freedom to examine and know why a certain decision is right and another wrong.

Referring to a person's intended decision, The Buddha repeatedly mentioned that knowledge would allow the person to decide correctly. While some contemporary teachers cited beliefs and social practices to justify their claims, the Buddha often asked, "Do they *know* their point as true and others' points as false?[1] Again, immediately after he rejected various methods of false reasoning, the Buddha encouraged his listeners to make the right choice based on knowledge, understanding, and wisdom.

"Know by yourself" is the term that clearly indicates the Buddha's point.[2] He asserted that one's acceptance or rejection of ideas and practices should depend on right knowledge. Undoubtedly, freedom to seek knowledge is the highest blessing that we may secure after putting aside fallacious reasoning.

The word "knowledge" may need further explanation. Blinded by false reasoning, some may see an assumption, hypothesis, intuitive urge, or hallucination as knowledge. However, as the Buddha specifically and unequivocally stated, knowledge means right understanding with evidence. The following dialogue between the Buddha and his visitor Bharadvaja clarifies what the Buddha specifically meant by knowledge:

Bharadvaja: Referring to the ancient mantras that come from oral tradition and textual preservation, some assert, "These are true; anything else is unwise." What do you, sir, say about this [argument]?

The Buddha: What do you say about this [question], Bharadvaja? Among these teachers, is there at least a single person who can say, "I know and I see these mantras as true, and anything else is unwise"?[3]

Again, according to the *Vasettha Sutta*, the concept of Brahma presents itself to be false because nobody has sensually experienced the existence of Brahma.[4] Overall, knowledge means clear and reliable evidence, particularly the evidence obtained through direct experience. To make the correct decision, we need to have knowledge about everything related to that decision.

ON RIGHT KNOWLEDGE

The *Kalama Sutta* summarizes one of the Buddha's most comprehensive teachings on knowledge. After identifying the fallacies in argument, this sutta elaborates on the kind of knowledge necessary for a person to make the most appropriate decisions.

As discussed in chapter 1, the members of the Sangha community preserved the huge collection of suttas through memory. In this process, they condensed the Buddha's lengthy teachings to a minimum for the sake of preservation. The *Kalama Sutta* seems to be one of the Buddha's teachings that went through rigorous summarization. In particular, a section on knowledge about decisions appears to have been a detailed explanation by the Buddha, and now contains only two paragraphs. Despite its brevity, however, this section in the *Kalama Sutta* clearly guides us toward the correct knowledge required for judicious decisions. Along with several other discourses, it presents a clear picture of what the Buddha meant by "right knowledge" about decisions.

FOUR FORMS OF RIGHT EVALUATION

The *Kalama Sutta* offers four forms of correct evaluation, all based on knowledge and understanding, to lead us toward right decisions. We should apply all four criteria in order to make a single wise decision. Let us take each of these evaluations for a detailed discussion.

RIGHT EVALUATION 1: WRONG MOTIVATIONS
LEAD TO WRONG DECISIONS

The Buddha claimed that, when a wrong inner urge motivates a person, the decision that follows fails to reflect the decision-maker's wisdom. Altogether, the Buddha recognized three such motivations: greed, malice, and illusion. Of course, these three motivations are the most common of all human motivations, but, as the Buddha explained, they all can easily corrupt a decision.

In the previous chapter, we discussed how illusion, the third motivation given above, tends to remove wisdom from a decision. There, we saw illusionary views restricting the individual's inner freedom and suppressing his or her rational thinking. In the present section, we will elaborate on how greed and malice, the other two motivations, tend to hamper the wisdom of the decision-maker.

How greed affects a decision adversely. To clarify how greed tends to make a decision unwise, we first need to have a clear picture of what *greed* means. For the reader's convenience, we have to select English equivalents for Pali terms while discussing the Buddha's teaching. Although the word *greed* serves that purpose, it fails to convey what the Buddha meant by several Pali words, which, of course, connect to, but go beyond, what we mean by *greed*.

On different occasions, the Buddha used such words as *lobha*, *raga*, *tanha*, and *mahaiccha* to mean this unwholesome motivation. *Lobha* may be defined as "insatiable desire for material objects or power." *Raga* basically refers to the desire for bodily satisfaction. *Tanha* means "the desire for possession and sensory satisfaction." *Mahaiccha* seems to suggest thinking and desiring beyond one's needs. The word *greed*, as used here, includes all these meanings. These different aspects of greed clearly obstruct human wisdom in a decision.

Obviously, uncontrolled desire for sensory satisfaction leads to irrational and harmful behavior. As a result, decisions made in a greedy spirit reveal no wisdom on the part of the decision-maker. Wrongful conduct, or *kamesu micchacara*, is the next reaction of the greed-dominated person. This reaction would almost always lead to unwholesome effects. "I have seen nothing other than greed to cause so many damaging effects," the Buddha once observed. "Greed is so harmful."[5]

Identifying some of these negative consequences, the Buddha again noted, "*Tanha* breeds sadness and suffering; *tanha* breeds fear."[6] Blinded by the burning desire to satisfy both body and mind, a greedy person may take falsehood as truth and make decisions that are devoid of wisdom. He or she fails to realize that suffering would be the eventual outcome of greed-motivated decisions. Clarifying the Buddha's teaching, his disciple Ananda remarked that, driven by greed, one would fail to differentiate between what is beneficial and what is harmful.[7] This weakness of the greedy person makes his or her decisions injudicious.

Violent actions and destructive, merciless behavior kindled by hunger for power demonstrate how greed further affects decisions. "The greedy thought, 'I will become powerful; power is important to me,' produces numerous evil and unwholesome effects," the Buddha said. "Overwhelmed by greed and devoid of self-control, one makes others suffer unjustly through punishment, imprisonment, destruction of wealth, character assassination, and banishment."[8]

We have only to look at some former world leaders—those who fell from grace—to see the truth of this statement. They destroyed nations, wiped out generations, and caused immeasurable suffering to humankind because they greedily sought power. Their decisions were proved to be wrong not only because their course of action consisted of huge blunders but also because they never found the happiness they were desperately looking for.

Moreover, unwholesome and unprofitable actions provoked by blind lust provide more evidence in favor of the Buddha's emphasis that a decision motivated by greed reflects little wisdom. "Uncontrollable lust causes mental blindness, blurred vision, and depleted wisdom," observed Ananda. Consequently, one who is driven by lust "commits unwholesome actions through words, deeds, and thoughts." These actions cause "harmful effects on oneself, on others, and on both oneself and others."[9] The damaging consequences produced by lust-driven decisions confirm the absence of wisdom in such decisions.

Overall, the Buddha clarified how greed, the uncurbed and unmanaged inner tendency for sensual pleasure and power, would drag people into unwise decisions. Blinded by their uncontrollable desire to please themselves and to raise their social standing, greedy people often tend to take falsehood as truth. Consequently, they make themselves unsuitable for rational decisions. The ineffectiveness and the impending harm of their actions attest to the absence of wisdom in their decisions.

How malice drains wisdom out of a decision. The term *malice,* again used for convenience, also represents a broad meaning. The Buddha used such words as *dosa* (hatred, ill will), *kodha* (anger), *upanaha* (grudge, ill will, enmity), and *aghata* (hurtfulness) to refer to this mental condition. All these words signify complex manifestations of a single human tendency: the urge and the effort to destroy any source of dissatisfaction and frustration. The Buddha explained how a decision motivated by this destructive tendency would fail to reflect the decision-maker's wisdom.

The Buddha observed a close connection between greed and malice—both tend to drain wisdom out of a decision in much the same way. When greed arises in the mind, malice also appears to further debilitate the individual's wise judgment. Both greed and malice give rise to inner blindness that prevents people from differentiating between what is beneficial and what is not. Both provoke actions that lead people to unhappiness. Both greed and malice jointly hamper the wisdom of people's decisions.

Apart from this hand-in-hand process, malice also plays its own harmful part in human decisions in many ways. In particular, malicious thoughts tend to implant a profoundly false belief in the human mind, the belief that hate-oriented actions can solve problems and resolve conflicts. Driven by this false conviction, people in conflicts continue to sharpen their techniques to hurt the opposition. In doing so, they only make an already unpleasant situation worse.

"Hatred can never be conquered by hatred," the Buddha taught.[10] Citing a parable to clarify this truth, he indicated how conflicts tend to gather momentum and cause increasing devastation as people rely on hate-oriented decisions to solve their conflicts.[11]

The Buddha's attitude toward war further confirms his assertion that a decision impelled by malice only produces unwholesome effects and, therefore, contains no rationality.[12] The warriors of the Sakiya and Koliya kingdoms decided to fight against each other in order to solve a dispute over the use of water resources. The Buddha intervened and urged the two clans to refrain from fighting. He made it clear that the problem could be solved not by fighting but by sharing the water resources so that both parties could feel satisfied. In other words, the Buddha suggested that anger and vengeful thoughts, the immediate inner motives for fighting, would cause suffering for both sides and distract people from arriving at rational conclusions.

The Buddha's poetic description of an angry person's mental and physical actions is still the best example of how a decision made under the influence of ill will goes against the wisdom of the decision-maker. A section of this beautiful and meaningful poem is quoted below. It will help us see how anger-driven decisions exhibit the decision-maker's absurdity rather than his or her sagacity.

> I address those who, in anger, commit
> Unjust acts that cause suffering.
> Listen!
>
> An angry person, always unpleasant,
> Dwells in sheer misery.
> Gaining profit, he regards it unprofitable;
> Causing harm through words and deeds,
> He ends up losing wealth.
>
> Intoxicated by the spirit of anger,
> He becomes a person of disgrace;
> Relatives, friends, and associates
> All alienate an angry person.

Anger brings loss; anger burns the mind;
Unknown to others, fear exists within.

Being angry, he doesn't see what is beneficial;
Conquered by anger, he falls into utter blindness.
He revels in evils as if they were good
But later suffers as if engulfed in fire.

He has no shame, no fear for evil acts;
He is devoid of respectful words.
When overcome by anger,
He has no inner support at all.

In anger one slays mother or father;
In anger one kills a holy person or any person.

An angry person can destroy the life
Of the one who gave and fed his own!

One is the dearest to oneself, but with anger
One kills oneself.[13]

This poem stresses that anger would suppress people's rational thinking, leading them to irrational behavior. Driven by anger, they use foul language and exhibit neither shame nor fear in committing unwholesome deeds. Sadly, anger makes them fall into dreadful blindness, urging them to destroy the lives of their own family members and other people alike. To make its blindness more complete, anger entices people to take their own lives, the dearest of all their possessions. In brief, anger negates wisdom in a decision because the indomitable strength of anger transforms a normal individual into a senseless rogue.

Obviously, malice—hatred, grudge-bearing, revengeful thoughts, anger, and so on—leads to a decision devoid of wisdom. Joined together with greed, it heightens its debilitating effects on human decisions. Malicious thoughts create the illusionary impression that problems can be solved through violence. Again, the same imbalanced state of mind baffles the decision-maker, dragging the person to totally irrational conclusions. This confusing and misleading mental process clearly indicates how malice eliminates wisdom from a decision.

RIGHT EVALUATION 2: ABSENCE OF WRONG MOTIVATIONS LEADS TO RIGHT DECISIONS

The Buddha saw the absence of wrong motivations as essential in order to bring wisdom into decisions. The meaning of this view is twofold. First, before making a decision, we should endeavor to make sure that our minds are not dominated by greed, malice, and illusion. Next, we should convince ourselves that the unwholesome motivations have been replaced by right thoughts. Again, since the "illusionary thought" has drawn sufficient attention in the previous chapter, we will now clarify the connection between wise decisions and the absence of greed and malice.

How absence of greed leads to right decisions. We have already seen how greed tends to make a person's decision unwise. Being the voracious desire for self-gratification, greed blinds a person's vision and drives him or her to irrational and unwholesome conclusions. In contrast, the absence of greed brightens one's wisdom, paving the way for "numerous wholesome effects."[14]

As the Buddha's disciple Ananda said, non-greed would establish mental calmness, safeguard individual morality, and enhance the ability to differentiate between beneficial and nonbeneficial actions.[15] In this manner, the absence of greed in the

mind prepares the background for an individual to make judicious decisions.

As various suttas consistently emphasize, mental calmness is
the foundation for wisdom. While greed breeds more desire,
similar to an all-conquering king's hunger for more lands
beyond the ocean,[16] subdued greed brings peace of mind. This
mental condition is a clear indicator of one's ability to make
rational decisions.

Notably, two characteristics in the mind that has subdued
greed contribute to the person's mental peace. First, inner suffering or an unsatisfactory state of mind, the companion of
burning desire, no longer disturbs the person. Second, dejec-
tion and frustration, the harbingers of greed-related pleasure-
seeking, no longer continue to harrow the person. As a result,
peacefulness settles in the mind, facilitating the person's ability
to decide on the actions that are beneficial to himself or herself
and to others.[17]

The following passage of the Buddha's teaching shows
another aspect of improved wisdom in a mind which has subdued greed. Such a mind guides a person's social and political
ascendancy in the most appropriate manner:

> Freed from greed, relieved from greed, and undisturbed
> by greed, a person who seeks power stops causing
> unjust suffering to others through punishment, impris-
> onment, destruction of wealth, abuse, or banishment.[18]

These crucial words convey an enlightening message. When
greed is subdued, respect for morality—a clear sign of wisdom—begins to shine within the individual.

The ability to differentiate between beneficial and nonbeneficial actions is the most noticeable skill that the absence
of greed implants in the individual. To sum up, "greed gone,

one sees what is beneficial to oneself, what is beneficial to others, and what is beneficial to both parties."[19]

How absence of malicious thoughts makes a decision wise. As previously discussed, the Buddha observed that both greed and hatred connect to influence human decisions in a negative way. Together, they rigorously suppress human rationality, thus inhibiting the wisdom in one's actions. The submergence of the two negative motivations, in contrast, jointly contributes to wise decisions.

On numerous occasions, the Buddha explained how this works. Similar to what non-greed does, the absence of hatred also brings about mental clarity and implants morality in the mind. This frame of mind improves the individual's ability to make the most appropriate decisions. As already mentioned, greed and malice, according to the Buddha's definition, are the two most dominant negative forces in the human mind. They darken the vision and impair the judgment. As both forces lose their grip on the mind, people regain their vision, and their rational thinking is restored.

From the Buddha's viewpoint, eradication of malicious thoughts is, in fact, the individual's highest achievement. Untainted by malice, the most harmful motivation, a decision should show more rationality, more wisdom. Basically, greedy and angry or malicious thoughts only depict a false picture about the benefits and harmful effects of one's decision.

The phrase "absence of malicious thoughts" does not, of course, suggest the necessity of having some kind of "blank" mind at the time one makes a decision. Rather, this phrase means the presence of compassion and respect as a requirement for a right decision. The absence of ill will (e.g., anger, hatred, vengefulness) does not leave the mind empty; rather, it allows love and compassion to pour in and fill the gap. Therefore, when malicious thoughts depart, loving-kindness takes their place to help evaluate the forthcoming decision.

How does loving-kindness provide such a strong support for correct decisions? To answer this question, we first need to focus on the meaning of the term "loving-kindness." Again, translations of the original Pali words are not perfect, and "loving-kindness" may convey the idea that one should somehow ignore one's own well-being and pay overwhelming attention to others' welfare as a criterion for rational decisions.

However, the Buddha's advice is that one should never concede one's own well-being to that of others: in fact, love and respect for oneself represent an essential part of loving-kindness. The rise of these feelings during the process of decision-making signifies a balanced and respectful evaluation of the benefits that a decision would offer to oneself and to others involved in the decision.

RIGHT EVALUATION 3: CONSEQUENCES OF A DECISION MAKE IT RIGHT OR WRONG

The Buddha consistently emphasized that, before we determine that a decision is right, it should also be evaluated in terms of its possible consequences. The most notable point in this emphasis is that correct motivation alone would not make a decision completely right. Besides ensuring the presence of wholesome motivations, the decision-maker should also consider the possible consequences of the decision.

Of course, reduced greed and ill will and cultivated loving-kindness lay the foundation for wise judgment. Still, the Buddha stressed that one should learn how to construct a rational argumentation upon that foundation in order to reach a rational conclusion.

Several suttas explain what the Buddha meant by the term "evaluation of an action according to the consequences." To complete this evaluation successfully, first we need to answer the following three questions carefully:

> Does the decision lead to my own well-being (atta
> sambita)?
> Does the decision lead to the well-being of others
> who are involved in the decision (parattha
> sambita)?
> Does the decision lead to the well-being of both
> myself and others involved (ubhayattha
> sambita)?[20]

We previously discussed the Buddha's assertion that one should never disregard one's own well-being. By urging his listeners to make decisions that would lead to their own well-being, the Buddha indicated that one should care about one's own success and happiness. Still, a lopsided decision that leads only to the decision-maker's well-being is not acceptable, either. The Buddha's view is that a decision should provide welfare not only for the decision-maker but also for those affected by the decision.

The Kalama Sutta indicates that the word "well-being" (sambita) contains a broad meaning. Three Pali words—atthaya, hitaya, and sukhaya—define the word "well-being." Atthaya and hitaya refer to the benefits that a decision brings to both the decision-maker and others. Sukhaya indicates happiness associated with a decision. The two words "benefit" and "happiness" seem difficult to separate. Yet, obviously, the Buddha used two different words because he noticed a difference between benefit and happiness.

We observe that a beneficial decision may not always cause happiness. Similarly, a decision that would bring immediate happiness may not be beneficial at all. What is important is to have a balanced evaluation of both the benefits and the happiness that a decision would bring to the decision-maker. But even though the Buddha defended self-benefit as a positive effect of a decision, he never admitted it to be the sole criterion.

Extreme forms of both selfishness and selflessness hinder wise judgment. Moderation, on the other hand, paves the way for wisdom.

RIGHT EVALUATION 4: ATTENTION TO THE VIEWS OF QUALIFIED PEOPLE LEADS TO RIGHT DECISIONS

The Buddha also explained that approval by the wise (*vinnu-pasattha*) and rejection or censure by the wise (*vinnugarahita*) are important tools for a person to judge the wisdom of a decision.[21] The Buddha insisted that we should apply this criterion when we decide to abandon something or to "accept and live accordingly."

The important question is, "Who is the qualified person?" The Pali word for "the qualified person" is *vinnu*. Interestingly, both *vinnu* and "know" derive from the same Sanskrit root *jhana*, which means "knowledge," "wisdom," or "education." A *vinnu* is translated as "the person who is intelligent, wise, or learned." In brief, those who possess the ability to reason wisely and to manage greed and malice are the wise people. Those who have expert knowledge in a certain field are the learned people. Importantly, however, if the learned person lacks wisdom, attention to that person's opinion can lead an individual into unwise decisions. A qualified person to depend on for decisions is one who possesses both knowledge and wisdom.

SUMMARY

Overall, the Buddha—having rejected fallacious argumentation—offered us the freedom to rationally evaluate a decision. Proper evaluation of both the intention and possible consequences of a decision paves the way for us to arrive at the most rational decisions. Attention to the views of qualified people also facilitates right decision-making.

The phrase "humanistic pragmatism," which suggests the practical usefulness of a decision to everybody involved, sums up the Buddha's values in decision-making. When evaluating a decision's effectiveness, we should consider both self-benefits and others' well-being. After all, *I* (any person) deserve the right to come to the ultimate decision; but *I* also must take responsibility for the consequences of that decision.

CHAPTER 12: WHAT NOT TO DO IN DAILY LIFE

Disciplined actions and disciplined words
are a blessing to the layperson.
                              The Buddha, *Sutta Nipata*

As discussed in the last two chapters, the Buddha introduced a complete set of criteria for evaluating decisions. Using the same criteria, he presented a list of eight wrongful actions that individuals should refrain from. This chapter will explore how we can avoid being driven by those impulses which, while natural and human, easily cause suffering.

In general, there are five main habits to refrain from, which are categorized as the Five Precepts. Many believe that the Five Precepts are simple, strict, and clear-cut rules. However, close observation of the Buddha's relevant teachings reveals that this belief is not always correct. The Five Precepts are often other than they appear, as the Pali wording of each precept does not always present it clearly. We will clarify what the Buddha taught about the Five Precepts, but first let us take each of the eight rules separately for an orderly discussion.

1. DO NOT DESTROY LIFE

Destruction of life is the first action the Buddha always asked his lay followers to refrain from. To understand this practice correctly, we first need to study the Pali term the Buddha used to convey this idea. He said *panatipata veramani* or *panatipata pativirato* to convey this advice. The words *veramani* and *pativirato* are usually translated as "refraining from."

However, *panatipata* is a compound word: *pana* (a living being)+*ati* (upon or toward)+*pata* (fall). This word can hardly be translated by a single English word. Precisely, it means attacking ("falling upon") any living being—as with either a weapon or physical force. Killing of both humans and animals is included in the first of the Five Precepts.

This advice found a preeminent position in the Buddha's teaching because he promoted great respect for life. To the Buddha, any form of life, especially human and animal life, were worthy of respect. Of course, life must depend on life for existence, but the Buddha never tolerated wanton destruction of life.

What kinds of killing are included in this precept? Close study of the *Sutta Pitaka* reveals that "destruction of life" includes the following forms of killing.

Unarguably, homicide is an act of destroying life, according to the Buddha. He never allowed individuals or groups to kill other humans. "In the same way I protect my life, others also value their lives, shun death, and look for happiness," the Buddha said. "Then how can one kill another?"[1] With this attitude, the Buddha always persuaded his community to respect fellow humans, and to never take their lives.

The Buddha's unequivocal rejection of homicide was based on several factors. First, he valued human life more than anything else. "To be born as a human being is a rare opportunity," he taught.[2] Human life is so precious in the Buddha's teaching because only a human being can attain Nibbana, the highest level of inner development. Next, the Buddha's philosophy never tolerated the fear and pain caused by killing. Considering these two factors, the Buddha clearly proclaimed that homicide would mean destruction of life.

Taking one's own life, according to the Buddha, is another manifestation of destroying life. He did not believe that suicide is a solution to human problems. What he emphasized throughout his speeches was the fruitfulness of human effort. Being an embodiment of great potential, a human being should learn not to run away from problems, but to challenge them. Killing oneself is an act of denying the enormous potential with which a human being is naturally endowed.

The Buddha was one of the first to stand against suicide. More importantly, he may be the first ever to *prevent* a suicide through compassionate intervention. When the teenage girl Rajjumala, who worked as a housemaid, tried to take her life, the Buddha volunteered to help her. She told the Buddha that she had lost interest in life because her employer continued to mistreat her. The Buddha comforted the child and talked to the lady who employed her. He found that the child had been treated as a slave. The Buddha eventually persuaded the lady to adopt Rajjumala as her own daughter.[3]

The Buddha identified suicidal tendencies as an imbalanced state of mind. He said, "Driven by illusion (*mucchita*), people cut themselves with swords, take poison, hang themselves, and throw themselves from rocks."[4] This statement further clarifies his position regarding suicide. Wise judgment is absent in a person who attempts to take his or her life. In the presence of inner disturbances, one should strive to gain wisdom, rather than take one's life.

Two examples in the *Sutta Pitaka*, however, stand out as unique exceptions.[5] The Buddha found no fault with two of his ordained disciples who committed suicide after developing incurable diseases and suffering from intense pain. These examples may open peripheral topics, but what is obvious is that the Buddha never encouraged suicide as a solution to human conflicts and inner problems. Killing oneself to escape problems is an act of destroying life.

Killing as a source of enjoyment can also be categorized as destruction of life, according to the Buddha's viewpoint. Compassionate Buddha never encouraged humans to express joy at the sight of a suffering animal. One day, on his way to the city of Savatthi, the Buddha saw a group of young children attacking a snake. He found that the motive behind the children's attack was to seek cruel pleasure by watching the snake suffer. The Buddha helped the children understand the cruelty of their act.

He made his point clear by saying, "Those who harm animals as a source of enjoyment would never find happiness."[6]

And animal sacrifice, according to the Buddha, belongs in the same category as destroying life. Killing animals to please deities was a prevalent practice during the Buddha's time. In these sacrifices, animals were tied and even hung during the long period of prayer before they were killed. Several suttas indicate that the Buddha vehemently objected to such sacrifices.

In the *Kutadanta Sutta*,[7] the Buddha cited a parable to emphasize the uselessness and cruelty of animal sacrifices. He noted that the ancient king Mahavijita made a great sacrifice to deities without animal bloodshed. "In that sacrifice, not a single ox, goat, fowl, or pig was slain," the Buddha said. "With ghee, oil, butter, milk, honey, and sugar," the great king was able to acquire the perfect blessing of the deities. Even the attendants to the harmless sacrifice of King Mahavijita "carried on their work without tears on their faces" since no animals were killed.

The Buddha made it clear that animal sacrifice is both a waste and an instance of human cruelty.

WHAT ABOUT KILLING FOR FOOD?

One of the perennial arguments regarding human ethics is whether killing is acceptable as a means of obtaining food. A steadily increasing number of people assert that animals should not be a source of food for humans. We will find the Buddha's position on this controversial topic interesting and useful.

The Buddha's opinion about eating animal flesh was clearly dependent on other relevant factors. His permission for bhikkhus to accept meat and fish if the animals were not specially killed for them bears witness to his position. Importantly, bhikkhus never prepared their own meals. They carried a bowl and walked from house to house once a day for alms. They had to accept what was given to them, which was almost always a portion of what the people had prepared for themselves.

With wildlife so abundant and human population so sparse, people in that society ate mostly meat. Bhikkhus had no choice but to eat what they received from people. This example suggests that human beings may depend on animal life for sustenance when no choice is available other than eating animal flesh.

An important sutta in the *Anguttara Nikaya* confirms the Buddha's position. In this sutta he advised lay followers to avoid dependence on animal flesh if they have physical strength (*viriya*).[8] This seems to likely indicate that one who has enough physical strength to work should engage in agriculture, rather than use easy methods of killing domesticated animals or trapping wild beasts for food. Not everyone needed to be a farmer, of course—one could use one's strength to do any appropriate work that provided one the means to buy or barter for the goods of the agriculturalists.

And so a sick, helpless person might set a snare to catch a wild animal; but after regaining strength, that person should return to work, cultivating land and such. Under normal conditions,

using animals as a source of food is wrong, but in desperate situations, the individual decision could be otherwise.

The Buddha cited an individual's lack of physical strength as
an acceptable reason to live on animal flesh, because that situation was obvious in his society. In other societies and situations, however, different causes would force people to survive
on animal flesh. People living close to the North Pole, for
instance, would hardly find any agricultural products to eat. As
a result, they inevitably have to kill and eat animals to survive.
The Buddha's words indicate that people who encounter such
unusual difficulties finding agricultural products may survive
on animal flesh rather than starve.

Nevertheless, the Buddha's teaching strongly suggests that
people ought not kill animals for food or buy animal flesh when
other food is abundant. Greed for animal flesh, particularly
when sufficient nutritious food is obtainable through harmless
methods, indicates encouragement of killing, according to the
Buddha's ethics.

2. DO NOT TAKE ANYTHING WRONGFULLY

The next don't-do habit, as it occurs in the Five Precepts, is
adinna+adana veramani, literally, "keeping away from seizing what
is not given." This precept is generally defined as abstaining
from stealing, but the Pali term certainly covers a broader
meaning than this conventional definition.

The phrase *adinna+adana* includes bribery, burglary, forceful
acquisition of property, invasion of somebody else's territory,
fraud, theft, or any other deceitful way of obtaining money,
material objects, or other benefits.

The Buddha observed that numerous forms of "taking what is
not given" were prevalent in his society. A household servant
would steal money or other objects from the house of employ-
ment. A housewife would cheat her husband over the family

wealth entrusted to her. Organized thieves would plunder towns and villages. A merchant would cheat a customer, a group of robbers would ambush travelers, and one who sought great fortune would take bribes. Obviously, all such manifestations of wrongful acquisition are included in this don't-do advice.

The key phrase that defines this wrongful practice is "taking by means of theft or stealing what is not given."9 The Buddha obviously urged his followers to refrain from taking any deceitful, corruptive, or forceful steps as a means to obtaining material success.

3. AVOID SEXUAL MISCONDUCT

The next daily observance the Buddha recommended to his lay followers was to avoid misconduct in sensory pleasure (kamesu micchacara veramani). Kamesu means "in any form of sensory satisfaction." Micchacara is a compound word that means "wrong conduct." This advice is meant to guide people's sensory satisfaction in such a way that their search for sensual pleasure should not be a burden to themselves and others.

Even though "misconduct" refers to any form of sensory satisfaction, it specifically focuses on human sexuality. As previously mentioned, the Buddha recognized sexuality as a powerful human urge. He remarked that both men and women would find no better sight, sound, smell, or touch than that of one to whom they are sexually attracted.10 The human urge for physical satisfaction being so predominant, the Buddha offered extra assistance for his lay followers to manage their desire.

Even though the Buddha did not categorize all forms of sexual misconduct in a single passage, close attention to his teaching helps us to identify the acts that he classified as sexual misconduct. We will briefly discuss each of these acts that he persuaded society to refrain from.

UNFAITHFULNESS

A committed relationship, as the Buddha recognized in the *Sigalovada Sutta*, is one in which both partners fulfill their duties and responsibilities toward each other. The Buddha suggested that both the male and the female in such a relationship should abstain from seeking other relationships.

However, the proposed faithfulness to each other seems conditional. A man or a woman is not destined to remain committed to his or her partner forever simply because he or she began a relationship with the other. One partner's irresponsibility and negligence of his or her own duty and obligation, including faithfulness, would allow the other partner to leave and seek a different relationship. The following statement of the Buddha sheds light on this idea:

> A wife should not disregard [*na atimannati*] a husband who displays enthusiasm, strives [*for success*], provides for the needs of his wife, and always takes care of her.[11]

This statement hints that commitment should be mutual. In the Buddha's society, men were responsible for accumulating wealth. The Buddha suggested that they had to be active and strive for success. They also had to use the wealth in order to take care of their wives and to provide comfort for them. A wife should not disregard such a dutiful husband.

The same quotation also implies a wife's rights to disregard a husband who habitually exhibits no interest in success, wastes his time, and neglects his duties toward her. *Atimannati*, the Pali word quoted above, has multiple meanings, such as "neglect," "disregard," and "despise." A wife might be free to find another life partner in cases where her husband blatantly ignores his duties toward her and the family.

Of course, the Buddha did not suggest that one might seek extramarital relationships when one's partner fails to be dutiful. Instead, he apparently meant that finding a dutiful partner would be better than remaining faithful to a person who would neglect his or her duties. The Buddha offered both men and women the freedom to leave uncommitted partners and to choose better persons.

Still, the Buddha maintained that, when one partner is dutiful and faithful, the other partner should also remain committed to the relationship. A person's involvement with others while being in a committed relationship means sexual misconduct, according to the Buddha.

SEDUCTION

Also, the Buddha specified that seduction—solicitation of sex through lies, false promises, and irrational appeals—should be categorized as sexual misconduct. In the *Veludvareyya Sutta*, the Buddha asked his lay community members to refrain from seduction as a part of their effort to avoid sexual misconduct. He asked men to compare their feelings to others' in the following manner: "I detest others who seduce my wife. In the same way, others would dislike my own seduction of their wives."[12] The Buddha explained that this comparison would facilitate their understanding of seduction as sexual misconduct.

FORCED SEX

Another aspect of sexual misconduct is the use of force to obtain sex. This form of sexual misconduct includes any sexual assault, such as uninvited sexual advances, harassment, and rape. The Buddha never permitted violence. Harmlessness should predominate over all human actions. Forced sex violates this most important principle.

The Buddha identified abstinence from forced sex as a sign of worldly progress for laypeople.[13] In his examples, the Buddha pointed at men as those who would commit such wrongful deeds. They would approach single or married women who are under the protection of others,[14] or force their victims to participate in sexual acts.[15] The Buddha advised people to abstain from such wrong deeds. Overall, he considered any forceful sexual behavior as sexual misconduct.

INCEST

Unsurprisingly, the Buddha also regarded incest as sexual misconduct. He did not tolerate incest even if such a sexual relationship was based on mutual consent.[16] The Buddha observed that abstaining from incest is a social rule, but he respected it for its benefits. He identified incest as a sign of human degeneration.[17] The Buddha urged his lay community to stay away from incest because doing so would contribute to both individual and social progress.

SEXUAL ABUSE OF MINORS

The Buddha considered sexual abuse of minors as another form of sexual misconduct. This idea is evident in the Buddha's remarks that those who abuse sexually immature people are lower than dogs.[18] To emphasize the baseness of child abusers, the Buddha mentioned that even male dogs would not mate with sexually immature females. Anybody who sexually abuses children violates an ethical code that even dogs respect.

OVERINDULGENCE IN SEX

The other form of sexual misconduct, as the Buddha saw it, was overindulgence in sex. For the layperson, the Buddha always emphasized moderation in all forms of sensory satisfaction. Self-indulgence is at one extreme; self-denial is at the other. The middle path is clearly applicable to the layperson's enjoyment of sexual pleasures as well. The Buddha's phrase "in right measure," which he specifically used to indicate moderate eating, can be extended to all forms of sensory satisfaction, including the satisfaction of sexual desires.

In a general sense, the phrase "overindulgence in sex" defies a simple definition. It can be engagement in multiple sexual relationships, overemphasis of sex with a single partner, or a keen search for different methods of sexual satisfaction. One's attitude toward sex seems to set the boundaries for moderation and indulgence. The erroneous view that constant gratification of sexual desires leads a person to happiness seems to be the attitude that takes a person beyond moderation.

Apparently, the Buddha did not maintain that reproduction is the only purpose of a sexual relationship between a man and a woman. Instead, he regarded such a relationship as a source of joy for a layperson. The Buddha's statement that "One should be happy (santuttho) with one's own wife, without seeking other women"[19] conveys this idea. The word santuttho includes a sexual connotation. The urge for sex is not something one should consistently suppress; it is something for a layperson to express. However, he or she should be aware of the limits that define moderation.

And what about premarital sex and homosexuality? We find no information about premarital sex and homosexuality in the Buddha's teachings. The most appropriate approach, therefore, is to evaluate both practices in terms of same general criteria the Buddha spoke of elsewhere. As previously discussed, unwholesome intention behind an action and the negative effects resulting from an action are the main criteria to be considered in evaluating an action.

One of the greatest concepts in Buddha's teaching was individual freedom of choice. A harmless substitution for the traditional male-female sexual relationship does not seem to contradict the Buddha's criteria of evaluating an action.

4. DO NOT SPEAK UNTRUTHS WITH WRONG INTENTION

The Buddha advised his lay community to refrain from speaking untruths that have their roots in the wrong intention. The phrase "wrong intention" is a key term in this precept. We need to examine our own thoughts to find out the motive behind speaking an untruth. If the motive is to gain unfair advantage or to cause any harm, that untruth is a lie.

The Pali term the Buddha constantly used to mean avoidance of telling lies was *musavada veramani*. This term is often translated as "refraining from telling lies," but this translation seems inadequate and even misleading. We need to know the connotative meaning of the word *musavada* to understand what the Buddha actually meant by this precept.

Even though the word *musavada* occurs hundreds of times in the *Sutta Pitaka*, the explanation of the term, similar to that of many others, is always brief. Nevertheless, certain passages in the suttas offer some clues as to what the Buddha meant by *musavada*. The following quotation is just one example:

> If someone destroys my welfare with lies, that act is unpleasant to me. If I do the same, my own act would be unpleasant to others.... One who reflects thus should refrain from *musavada*.[20]

This quotation indicates that false speech is characterized by the speaker's intention to cause destruction of others' welfare. Unwholesome intention and the impending harmful effects are the decisive factors of false speech. Various suttas indicate that many kinds of false speech cause harm and, therefore, should be avoided. We will briefly refer to some of these categories.

FALSE REPORT

False report is one obvious form of lying that the Buddha asked his followers to refrain from. In the Buddha's society, numerous thinkers were ardently campaigning for followers. Some supporters of different schools of thought intentionally distorted a speech given by an opposing leader in a sinister plan to harm the reputation of such a leader. On several occasions, the Buddha found his own speeches being intentionally misinterpreted to harm his reputation. He called such distortion a harmful act that should be avoided.

FALSE ACCUSATION AND PERJURY

False accusation and perjury are two more manifestations of lying that the Buddha wanted his listeners to avoid. The *Mahasihanada Sutta*[21] provides an example of false accusation that the Buddha disapproved of. He remarked that in a public or private dealing with somebody else's wrongdoing, one should speak about "only what had happened."[22] He identified perjury as a practice that would cause harm to the speaker, as well as to others. Both practices are lies that people should do away with.

FALSE PROMISE

Making false promises to gain advantage is another form of lying that the Buddha regarded as harmful, and requested his followers to abstain from. He recognized those who provide mere lip service as liars of that sort.[23] One who might give various excuses to avoid one's duty to a friend despite one's ability to fulfill such a duty would also belong to the same category of liars.[24] Some others might "deceive a Brahmin, an ordained person, or any clergyman by telling lies."[25] The deception in this case would be the intention of the pupil to learn from the holy person after giving false promises about fulfilling his or her duty. In all these cases, the ulterior motive of deception is the sign that characterizes a speech as false.

FALSE SELF-PRESENTATION

The Buddha remarked that false self-presentation is another form of lying from which his followers should refrain. This false speech includes giving false information about one's qualifications, skills, achievements, and conduct in order to gain undeserved advantages. Exaggeration of one's spiritual qualifications would be another example of false self-presentation. Any effort to hide one's own wrongdoings and to present oneself as a virtuous person also belongs to false self-presentation. According to the Buddha's observation, inadequate personality development would be a reason for such behavior.

SKILLFUL SPEAKING OF UNTRUTH

Speaking untruth, from the Buddha's viewpoint, would be acceptable as long as such an act follows a wholesome intention and serves a wholesome purpose. In fact, the word *lie* would be inappropriate to mean a false statement thus made. The Buddha himself used both "apparent" and "actual" untruth as a rhetorical technique to guide people toward wholesome decisions and actions (and silence, of course, was another technique the Buddha used to postpone speaking the truth when it would be unhelpful to hear).

For instance, Kesi, a horse trainer, told the Buddha that he (Kesi) would kill the horses that were untamable. The Buddha immediately replied that he (the Buddha) would also "kill" the people who would never succeed in achieving inner progress. Stunned by the Buddha's reply, Kesi retorted that he wondered how the Buddha, who taught loving-kindness, would kill people. The Buddha then said that his use of the word "killing" meant "leaving out."[26] In other words, he made an apparently untrue statement to convince his listener that sending the untamable horses back to the jungle would be a better choice than killing them.

Moreover, evidence clearly supports instances when he intentionally presented untruth as another means to wait for the right time to speak the truth.

One clear example is the Buddha's assurance to Gotami that her dead child's life could be restored. For the baby's treatment, he asked Gotami to bring a handful of mustard seeds from a family in which no death had taken place. The Buddha observed that telling the truth (that the dead child's life could not be restored) would be harmful to Gotami since she was so distraught at the time. With that awareness, the Buddha used actual untruth as a means to put off telling the truth. That approach led Gotami to eventually accept her child's death in a spiritually beneficial way.

5. DO NOT ALLOW ALCOHOL TO CAUSE PHYSICAL AND MENTAL IMBALANCE

This don't-do habit has given rise to much controversy. Some argue that this precept means total abstinence from all kinds of intoxicants. Others believe that it means controlled use of alcohol. Let us examine this precept closely to find out its most probable meaning.

The Pali term for this controversial precept is *suramerayamajjapamadatthana veramani*. "Abstaining from" is the meaning of *veramani*, but the first word of this precept is tricky and ambiguous. It is a compound term with five words joined together. *Sura*, *meraya*, and *majja* seemingly refer to three kinds of intoxicating drinks that people used during the Buddha's time. *Pamada*, a technical Pali word meaning "heedlessness," "inattention," or "delay," suggests the drinker's inability to do the right act or to make the right decision. *Thana* has several meanings, but in this precept it means "able to cause." The entire precept thus means "abstention from intoxication that would cause mental imbalance and physical torpidity."

A subtle ambiguity lies hidden in the translation, as well as in the original precept. Did the Buddha urge his lay community to refrain from the very practice of drinking alcohol, which would generally cause mental imbalance and physical torpidity? If not, did he want them to refrain only from *excessive use* of alcohol, also a practice that would cause those same effects? In other words, did the Buddha regard the given dangers as inherent to liquor itself, or to the excessive intake of liquor?

The Buddha never imposed strict rules for his community members. Some traditions during the Buddha's time held that alcohol was a divine drink, others that alcohol was essential for happiness and health. Given this social background, we might find it difficult to imagine that the Buddha strongly persuaded his lay followers to do away with alcohol completely. In his advice to Sigala, the Buddha mentioned that one should not indulge in alcohol because such indulgence would cause one to get sick and to lose wealth.[27] Thus, it seems the Buddha was more concerned about the effect on his lay followers' mental and physical behavior, and the loss of wealth caused by alcohol.

Apparently, the Buddha recommended this precept to prevent his lay followers' excessive and habitual use of alcohol, or, in other words, alcohol abuse. All evidence considered, Pali scholars Rhys Davids' and William Stede's translation of the precept in the *Pali-English Dictionary*—"abstaining from any state of indolence arising from the use of intoxicants"—seems more acceptable.

DRUG ABUSE

We find no information in the suttas about drug abuse because such a practice was not present in the Buddha's society. Nevertheless, as it is practiced today, drug abuse is similar to alcohol abuse, and the Buddha would have unequivocally asked his lay disciples to refrain from it.

Interestingly, the word *abuse* indicates the violation of one of the Buddha's most important rules for lay life, the rule of avoiding extremes. Using drugs for medical purposes is the right way to use them. Taking drugs for illusionary sensory satisfaction is an instance of exceeding the limits of proper use.

Misuse of drugs also goes against the Buddha's general criteria of evaluating an action. We have previously discussed how intentions behind an action, and also its consequences, jointly decide its effectiveness or invalidity. In drug abuse, we find neither wholesome intention nor wholesome effects.

6. DO NOT USE WORDS TO DIVIDE PEOPLE

Avoidance of words that divide people is the next don't-do habit the Buddha promoted among his followers. The Pali term for the word that causes division is *pisunavaca*. *Pisuna* means "malicious, slanderous, spiteful." *Vaca* suggests speech. Together, *pisunavaca* means "the use of language to split relationships."

Telling lies may also cause division among people, but a lie and a *pisunavaca* are different. Notably, a *pisunavaca* is a true or slightly exaggerated statement aimed at damaging a relationship. The Buddha explained that "telling there what one heard here" and "telling here what one heard there" characterize the speech that would cause division among people.[28]

The Buddha identified himself as a "promoter of unity through words."[29] Similarly, he instructed his disciples to "be fond of unity, to promote unity, and to use words to cause unity."[30] He insisted that his followers should avoid any form of speech that would threaten unity among people.

7. REFRAIN FROM USING HARSH LANGUAGE

In chapter 8, we referred to this habit as a prerequisite for healthy relationships. Avoiding harsh language is so important that the Buddha advised his lay followers to always be careful about how they spoke.

According to the *Veludvareyya Sutta*, the Buddha's lay followers should avoid harsh language because such language would be "unpleasant and unfriendly to the listener."[31] Soft words, in contrast, are "pleasing to the ear and go straight to the hearts of all."[32] The Buddha strongly believed that verbal abuse would never help people to improve their behavior or to establish healthy relationships.

8. AVOID SENSELESS TALK

Finally, the Buddha urged his listeners to practice "avoidance of senseless talk" as a daily habit. The phrase "senseless talk" covers a broad meaning. Its original Pali word is *samphappalapa*. Even though we have translated this Pali word as "senseless talk," we need to discuss the Buddha's explanation of *samphappalapa* to understand its complete meaning.

The Buddha identified six kinds of speech as belonging to senseless talk.[33] He advised his listeners to be mindful that their words would not belong to those categories. We will briefly discuss how speech becomes a *samphappalapa* or meaningless talk.

WORDS SPOKEN AT THE WRONG TIME

An expression inappropriate to the occasion is an example of senseless speech, according to the Buddha's explanation. We previously discussed how the Buddha identified himself as one who spoke at the right time. He explained that, to make a speech, conversation, or comment meaningful, the speaker should say it at the right time (*kalavadi*).

WORDS THAT CONTAIN UNTRUTH OR EXAGGERATION

Words that present false information as true belong to the category of senseless speech. Also included in this category are exaggeration and fabrication of news, events, occurrences, consequences, and accusations. The Buddha's advice is that one should present true information (*bhutavadi*) in order to convince the listener.

WORDS THAT BRING NO BENEFIT

Words that bring no benefit to the speaker or to the listener also belong to the group of senseless words. Self-display through words, long-winded conversations about others, and discussion of meaningless topics are some of the examples of unprofitable speech. We may be engaged in such conversations for hours but find no meaning in them. The opposite is the use of profitable words, or *atthavadi*, as the Buddha called it.

WORDS THAT LEAD THE LISTENER TO UNWHOLESOME THOUGHTS AND CONDUCT

The Buddha further indicated that words persuading the listener to unwholesome thoughts and actions also belong to *samphappalapa*. Mainly, manipulative language fits into this group. Such language may corrupt the listener's mind and appeal to his or her negative emotions. Overwhelmed by the power of such words, the listener would develop greed and ill will and commit harmful deeds. The Buddha advised that words should encourage people toward wholesome thoughts and actions (*dhammavadi*) instead of leading them in the opposite direction.

WORDS THAT THREATEN THE LISTENER'S SELF-DISCIPLINE

Similar to words used for unwholesome persuasion are words that lead to the breakdown of self-discipline. Here, the Buddha drew attention to the danger of using language as a means to lead the listener toward undisciplined actions. Words that persuade people to break rules and develop harmful habits may be included in this category of senseless words. The opposite of this practice is the use of words to promote the listener's self-discipline (vinayavadi).

WORDS THAT EXPRESS TRITE AND SHALLOW IDEAS

Finally, when words express ideas that lack originality, novelty, and depth, such words do not benefit a listener and also belong to the category of senseless speech. In contrast, the Buddha mentioned that words should express important views and ideas (nidhanavati vaca), which do not belong to the category of senseless speech.

According to the Buddha, any verbal expression that fits any of these six descriptions is a samphappalapa, or senseless speech. Such expressions are both useless and harmful, and accordingly, the Buddha advised his lay followers to reflect upon their speech before they spoke.

SUMMARY

The eight don't-do habits discussed in this chapter are the most important daily practices for the layperson. Even though the last three habits discussed above are not included in the Five Precepts, the Buddha frequently emphasized the importance of their daily practice for the lay community. He prescribed these habits because they would enable his lay followers to develop their external behavior—physical and verbal actions—to the best of their capabilities. That individual development, in turn, would contribute to the progress of society.

CHAPTER 13: DEVELOPING AN ATTRACTIVE PERSONALITY

Actions [words, deeds, and thoughts] determine
whether a person is well developed or not.
Wisdom illuminates his or her character.
The Buddha, *The Numerical Discourses*

Personality development is not merely a peripheral topic, but a focal point in the Buddha's teaching. A main objective of our life should be to develop our personalities to the highest level. To enable his followers to achieve this objective, the Buddha identified the characteristics that differentiate properly developed personalities from those that are inadequately developed. He examined why some people improve slowly while others achieve a fast and thorough improvement. Above all, he revealed techniques that allow his disciples to construct attractive personalities. This chapter focuses on the Buddha's techniques for personality development and discusses these points in detail.

First, however, to facilitate our understanding of the Buddha's recommendations, let us look at the criteria for personality evaluation employed at the time. The Buddha observed that his society was using a number of irrational measurements to rate people as higher or lower. When Sonadanda visited the

Buddha, he summed up those weak criteria to explain his own assessment of others. The most important requirements for a strong personality, he told the Buddha, would be fulfilled by one's birth into a noble family, knowledge of sacred texts, handsomeness, fair complexion, and a stately appearance.[1]

These widely held beliefs would, however, clearly sideline the more worthwhile criteria of an attractive personality. The Buddha not only rejected such weak building-blocks of personality but also introduced the solid values that would make an individual genuinely admirable and attractive.

GREAT PERSONALITIES ARE MADE, NOT INHERITED

The Buddha's central point regarding personality is that great personalities are made, not inherited:

> Birth does not make one a respectable person; one's action alone makes one a respectable person.[2]

The word *birth* refers to anything one might inherit: family background, wealth, physical appearance, race, caste, and so on. These factors provide only fragile criteria with regard to personality evaluation.

Action, by contrast, grants one solid material with which to construct an exceedingly attractive personality. Action's broad meaning is explained by the Buddha: "An action means what is done intentionally through words, deeds, and thoughts."[3] Throughout the *Sutta Pitaka*, it is clear that action includes our external as well as internal behavior patterns; and that, in order to develop an admirable personality, we should constantly modify our physical actions, words, and thoughts.

By affirming our ability to shape our behavior, the Buddha also gave us the responsibility to develop our personalities. Some forms of behavior, of course, might be inborn or "based on *kamma*." Still, the human ability to influence inborn behavior holds a prominent position in the Buddha's teaching. It may be impossible to change ourselves completely into altogether different people. Nevertheless, with self-awareness and observation, we may drastically improve our behavior and achieve more pleasing personalities.

Close analysis of the Buddha's process of personality development shows that it consists of the following three steps:

Step 1: Reflect upon and identify your own behavior
Step 2: Evaluate your own behavior
Step 3: Adjust and improve behavior

Let us examine each of them separately.

STEP 1: REFLECT UPON AND IDENTIFY YOUR OWN BEHAVIOR

The first step toward developing an admirable personality is to reflect upon and identify one's own behavior. We need to look into our own words, deeds, and thoughts and clearly recognize them. "An action with the body, speech, and mind should be done after repeated reflection," the Buddha taught. "It [self-reflection] is similar to a man or a woman looking into a clear mirror or a bowl of clear water. If the person sees dust or a blemish on his or her face, he or she strives to get rid of it."[4] So, self-reflection means a true effort to look into our own "actions" with the hope of modifying our behavior.

For some of us, this task is the hardest. We may exhibit expert skill in exposing others' weaknesses, but find it extremely difficult to detect our own. As the Buddha said:

One sees others' weaknesses very easily but finds it very difficult to see one's own. One can expose others' mistakes just as a winnower blows away chaff from grain. Yet one hides one's own mistakes just as a hunter camouflages himself with small branches and leaves.[5]

The Buddha's words elucidate our failure to observe our own weaknesses and reflect on our behavior. This hampers the process of adding pleasant qualities to our personalities and is the main reason why our personality development may stagnate.

Inability to recognize one's own mistakes or weaknesses is the most obvious characteristic of a *bala*, a technical word meaning "inadequately developed person."[6] Having failed at the initial stage, such a person shows little ability to improve his or her behavior.

The Buddha cited angry resistance and denial as common forms of escapism that prevent people from seeing their faulty behavior. The *Bala Vagga* in the *Anguttara Nikaya* consistently emphasizes this point. Upon recognizing a mistake, such people "show agitation, anger, and denial" instead of acceptance.[7] Inevitably, such individuals fail to genuinely reflect on their behavior.

These forms of self-defense are either absent or minimal in those who tend toward true self-reflection. Such people do not hide their faulty behavior "as a hunter camouflages himself with small branches and leaves." With sincerity and courage, they succeed in detecting the various traits in their characters.

The *Anumana Sutta* mentions the fact that close and honest self-investigation is the key to identifying traits that would otherwise go unnoticed. The Buddha instructed, "Self should be reflected upon self in this manner: Do I disparage others and exalt myself [while communicating]?"[8] The same sutta cites over fifteen characteristics, both wholesome and unwholesome, to be reflected upon in a similar way. Among these are the presence of immoral desires, the growth of jealousy within, and angry reaction to suggestions. This reflection would help one to "find the presence of unwholesome states [faulty behavior] that one must strive to get rid of," and the wholesome states that one should improve.⁹ So, genuine self-reflection leads us to right self-understanding, the next important step to self-adjustment.

In the Buddha's teaching, self-reflection leading to self-understanding is a vital phase in self-improvement. Genuine reflection on our own words, deeds, and thoughts allows us to identify our behavior. With the ability to reflect on our own internal and external behavior, we correctly recognize our actions and thoughts. As explained in the *Satipatthana Sutta*, the honest observer "sees lustful thought as lustful thought...and hateful thought as hateful thought."¹⁰ This kind of unbiased, impartial identification of our own words, deeds, and thoughts is the basic objective of self-reflection.

STEP 2: EVALUATE YOUR OWN BEHAVIOR

The Buddha explained that self-evaluation should follow self-reflection. While self-reflection facilitates the detection of various individual characteristics, correct self-evaluation takes us further: it allows us to measure the value of these traits. This step is important because we also need to measure what we have observed within ourselves. Such a measurement would help us to decide whether a certain behavior we exhibit is pleasant or unpleasant to others.

This phase, again, may mislead us. We may quickly judge others' unpleasant behavior as wrong and repulsive but our own wrong actions as pleasant and relevant. For instance, when others dominate a conversation, we might say that they are listening to their own voice, but when we speak too much, we believe, of course, that we are providing very useful information and instructions. When others express anger, they exhibit rude behavior, but our own angry outburst is the most appropriate response in the situation. These self-favored conclusions indicate that correct self-evaluation can be tricky and needs careful observation.

The *Sutta Pitaka* introduces the following methods for successful self-evaluation.

EXAMINE YOUR RESPONSE TO OTHERS' BEHAVIOR

Awareness of our own response to others' behavior, from the Buddha's point of view, is a dependable approach for evaluating others' response to our own behavior. According to this method, first we need to examine the behavior patterns of various individuals. Importantly, this examination does not mean we should interfere with what others do. Rather, it means we should evaluate our own behavior in the light of others' actions. We may select different people and silently observe and evaluate their notable behavior patterns. For example, the Buddha said:

> That person who praises himself or herself and disparages others is displeasing and disagreeable to me. Similarly, if I praise myself and disparage others, I would also be displeasing and disagreeable to others.[11]

We are more likely to misjudge if we try to evaluate our own behavior independently. A comparative evaluation, like the one the Buddha modeled in this example, offers us a great opportunity to determine social reaction to our own behavior.

The Buddha cited a large number of human characteristics, either admirable or contemptible, to be observed and evaluated in this manner. As exemplified in the quotation given above, we may first detect the presence of these behaviors in different individuals and then examine our own inner response to such behavior. If we deem these actions to be unpleasant, our own display of similar behavior will also earn the same negative response from society. On the other hand, if we tend to admire a certain behavior of others, our own adoption of similar behavior would also receive a similar appreciation from society.

IDENTIFY THE MENTAL STATES THAT CAUSE YOUR PLEASANT AND UNPLEASANT BEHAVIORS

Recognition of the mental states that prompt pleasant and unpleasant behaviors is another way to evaluate our actions. According to this approach, we need to examine the background of our behaviors and detect the urge behind them.

The Buddha identified all human actions as originating from six common sources: desire for sensory satisfaction, a destructive urge, illusion, generosity, compassion, and right understanding. The first three of these mental states can trigger unpleasant actions while the other three bring about pleasant behavior. Our ability to identify these mental states during an action helps us differentiate between what is pleasant and what is unpleasant.

A question such as "Why do I want to do this or say this?" would facilitate the detection of the motive behind an action. For instance, when a strong urge persuades us to talk about ourselves, we might pause for a moment to ask what the inner motive would be. An honest observation would perhaps reveal that a futile effort to gain power over our listeners would be the actual motive. In this case, we are urged by greed, an unwholesome motive that manifests itself in different forms. Talking about ourselves, of course, is not always an effort to gain power. Still, words, as well as actions, can often emerge from our inner desire to be more powerful. Mindfulness about the motive behind an action clearly helps us to evaluate the forthcoming actions.

EXAMINE THE SUITABILITY OF YOUR ACTIONS

An evaluation of the appropriateness of our actions toward certain persons and in certain situations is another useful way to assess our behavior. The Buddha remarked that, even though he knew something to be true, he would not say it at the wrong time.[12] Furthermore, he made a clear distinction between natural and rational behavior. The inner urge to do something is a natural force of behavior. Ability to evaluate the consequences of an action means the use of rationality. A person expecting to develop pleasant behavior should use the power of reasoning to evaluate his or her actions instead of giving in to instinct. The Buddha's following words clarify this point:

> When you are desirous of doing something through speech, you should reflect thus. Is this action unskilled? Does it lead to anguish? Is its result anguish...for myself and others? Does this action show my inner skill or lead to happiness...for myself and others?[13]

In everyday communications, we may have many "desirous" actions: to talk about our own achievements, to help others correct their behavior problems, or to say "Shut up!" to a grumbler. However, what positive effects should we expect by doing so? Unwholesome consequences lurk behind most of these "desirous" actions. Undoubtedly, we would earn a low personality evaluation from our listeners since our behavior would appear unpleasant to them. An assessment of our actions in terms of their effects would avoid a negative reaction from the listener.

One may argue that the truth is the truth, and that we should speak it irrespective of the occasion and the nature of the audience. However, the Buddha explained that speaking the truth to the wrong person or at the wrong time would cause a negative reaction. Therefore, we need to examine the suitability of our words before we decide to speak. The same measurement should be applied to evaluate other forms of actions as well.

STEP 3: USE SELF-EVALUATION TO ADJUST AND IMPROVE BEHAVIOR

So far, we have discussed self-reflection and self-evaluation, the two gradual and connected steps toward developing one's personality. The final phase of this improvement process is self-adjustment.

Self-evaluation gives us a clear picture of where improvement and adjustment are necessary. Now we can acquire the qualities that make us more pleasant to others and maintain those pleasant qualities we have already acquired. To clarify this step, the Buddha's disciple Sariputta explained the Buddha's words:

> It [self-improvement] is similar to the thinking of a young man or woman who has checked his or her reflection in a clear and pure mirror or in a bowl of clear water. If the person sees dust or a blemish on his or her face, he or she strives to get rid of it. If the person sees no dust or blemish, he or she feels happy and thinks, "Indeed, it is good for me; I am clean."
>
> Similarly, if you, while reflecting, see unwholesome states, you should strive to get rid of them. If you see they no longer exist, you should be delighted, and determined to maintain the developed states.[14]

Effort plays a key role in helping us to develop and retain pleasant qualities. Just as a young person is careful about his or her appearance, we need to be careful about our own behavior. If elated with our own beautiful actions, we could still make some effort to improve. If disappointed with unpleasant actions, we could make a determined effort to curb them. Without such effort, the chances of acquiring an attractive personality are remote.

In a society in which people look for easy success and instant results, the word "effort" might seem unappealing. But the Buddha, himself, saw no instant achievement in the matter of personality development. As with most success, developing a pleasing personality requires individual effort. This does not mean that we withdraw from our other work to concentrate on personality development alone. A few simple but productive habits will yield excellent results:

PRACTICING IMITATION AND ELIMINATION

The Buddha constantly praised imitation and elimination as greatly effective practices for developing an admirable personality. Imitation means following others' example and making an effort to acquire their attractive behavior. Elimination means refraining from following the example of others' unpleasant behavior and actually striving to leave out such behaviors. Having already learned to observe others' behavior, we now practice right evaluation which allows us to decide what is to be followed or left out. Here is an example:

> "That person who is stubborn and arrogant is disagreeable and displeasing to me. If I were stubborn and arrogant, I would also be disagreeable and displeasing to others." When you gain this knowledge, you must make up your mind and think, "I will not be stubborn and arrogant."15

The behavior of people in society constantly highlights characteristics that we need to adopt or reject. As spectators, we can evaluate this behavior and constantly change and modify our own, thus making us more acceptable to others.

We might argue that we are very independent and capable of learning by ourselves, and that we don't need to imitate others. In the Buddha's teachings, of course, self-reliance is an admirable characteristic. Realistically, however, no human being can improve his or her behavior without observing others. This is, in fact, a lifelong process that we all follow without even realizing it. The Buddha simply instructed us to imitate or eliminate behaviors selectively, after observing and evaluating carefully.

PRACTICING SELF-RESTRAINT

The Buddha taught that, like imitation and elimination, self-restraint, or *sila*, brings further self-adjustment.

Self-restraint simply means grappling with the tendency to exhibit unpleasant and unsuitable behaviors. When unwholesome mental states arise, self-restraint successfully stops us from displaying the consequent behaviors. It again comes to the rescue when our desired actions are unsuitable. It is important, however, not to define self-restraint as "suppression," or the forceful and painful hiding of behavior. With self-reflection and self-evaluation as its forerunners, self-restraint emerges from right understanding of our behavior and not as a forceful suppression of actions.

For example, when we restrain ourselves from reacting angrily, self-reflection and self-evaluation have already given us a clear understanding of our angry feelings. While an angry expression might be a natural reaction, mindfulness of our unwholesome mental state tells us it would hardly be pleasant. Right knowledge allows us to restrain unpleasant behavior without force or pain.

In some sense, self-restraint means gaining the upper hand over "natural" behavior. We may think naturally, but we need to behave rationally in order to develop an attractive personality. Self-restraint paves the way to that end.

By focusing on our external behavior, these practices help us to cultivate pleasant actions and weed out unpleasant ones.

STRIVING FOR INNER DEVELOPMENT

The Buddha also emphasized inner development as a unique step in acquiring pleasing qualities. "When mind is protected," he taught, "you protect all of your actions." [16] The fully developed person is one who improves not only external behavior but also thoughts, feelings, and attitudes. [17] Here, the word "protection" means to shield against the disturbances that affect our inner peace.

Enhancement of external behavior patterns is an essential but inadequate step in developing an admirable personality. Pleasant words and deeds, of course, make us socially acceptable; but improvement of attitudes and thoughts more clearly confirms our social acceptability. "Actions and words originating from a developed mind bring happiness," the Buddha stated. [18] In order to develop our personality to the best possible level, we need to work on our inner development.

On the one hand, the development of external behavior, itself, contributes to inner development. When we acquire new external behavior patterns, we tend to internalize them. When we use pleasant words, for example, we begin to feel we should continue using them. The Buddha highlighted this point by citing the connection between *sila* (behavior development) and *panna* (wisdom). We fail to develop wisdom if we fail to develop our verbal and physical behavior. Thus, external behavior development facilitates inner development.

For inner development itself, the Buddha recommended useful techniques, or *bhavana*, which prepare us inwardly to be in accord with our modified outer behavior. For instance, saying to someone "I am sorry to hear you are in trouble" indicates improved external behavior. But to actually feel compassion toward this troubled person indicates inner development.

The most effective way to improve our inner development is to enhance the loving-kindness and wisdom within us. Right behavior without right thoughts may be helpful in constructing an admirable personality; but right behavior *with* right thoughts is essential to a more complete personality.

Important techniques for inner development, or *bhavana*, are discussed in the next chapter, which focuses on happiness. Ultimately, however, these topics are so interrelated that we can hardly separate them. And after all, improved inner behavior supports the improvement of personality that is so crucial to our happiness and peace.

SUMMARY

The Buddha's teachings help us to develop the kind of charming characteristics that earn appreciation and respect. His methodical approach to personality development consists of three steps: self-reflection, self-evaluation, and self-adjustment.

Personality development refers to both the modification of our external behavior (words and deeds) and the improvement of our internal behavior (thoughts, feelings, and attitudes). We can modify our words and physical actions through imitation, elimination, and self-restraint. Inner development is possible through *bhavana* methods, which are popularly known as meditation.

CHAPTER 14: LASTING HAPPINESS

Indeed we live happily. In the midst of
worried people, we live free from worry....
Happiness is the greatest wealth.

The Buddha, *Dhammapada*

The trek through the thirteen chapters of this book now
brings us to the all-important topic: lasting happiness.
The immeasurable importance of this topic lies in one
simple truth: nothing that contributes to our success—wealth,
family, career, or any other achievement—serves any purpose
if it fails to make us happy. In our striving for success, happiness
is the greatest achievement. As the Buddha said, "I see no other
important acquisition for a person than happiness."[1]

THE GREATEST WEALTH

The Buddha repeatedly urged us to search for a stable and
intense form of happiness—and to find it and keep it with us so
that our successes become genuinely meaningful.

There are several powerful reasons to trust the Buddha's ability to lead us to this end. His sole endeavor throughout his life
was to find a lasting happiness; and, after considerable trial and
error, he proclaimed he had done so. The most reliable sources

indicate that the Buddha's words, deeds, and thoughts all reflected a consistent and intense happiness.

When, upon observing the Buddha's simple life, one visitor wondered whether he had rejected happiness, the Buddha replied: "If there are any individuals in this world experiencing happiness, I am undoubtedly one of them."[2] In the same sutta, he stated that he was happier than most people who possessed material wealth and power.

Moreover, unlike some of his contemporaries, the Buddha did not make himself suffer in order to experience happiness at some later time in life. He was happy throughout his life—thus highlighting his credibility as a reliable guide to our own happiness.

His disciples' joyfulness further justifies the Buddha's ability to lead us to happiness. In two ancient books, the *Theragatha* and the *Therigatha*, the poetic statements of the Buddha's male and female disciples are pervaded with happiness. These disciples were not living in luxury or enjoying expensive material possessions. But they possessed one thing in common: great happiness.

Thousands of disciples were successfully guided to happiness by the Buddha, and we can be confident that his instructions will do the same for us—if we follow them. Addressing his first group of bhikkhus, the Buddha said:

> Go earnestly from place to place for the benefit the many, for the happiness of the many, explaining to people the teaching that is excellent at the beginning, excellent in the middle, and excellent at the end.[3]

The presence of the word "happiness" here indicates the Buddha's ultimate objective in asking his disciples to take his message to "the many." He earnestly intended to make people happy, and he knew that his teachings could serve that purpose.

What's more, we can even find corroboration of this in current science. In a widely publicized news item, global media such as BBC and CNN reported on two separate studies done in late 2003 in American universities, pertaining to the happiness of Buddhist practitioners. And according to these reports, researchers found evidence suggesting that followers of the Buddha's teachings are actually happy—happier, in fact, than most.

New scanning techniques revealed that "certain areas of the brain light up constantly" in those who practice Buddhist meditation[4] and these seem to be associated with positive emotions and pleasant moods. Researchers at the University of California San Francisco Medical Center said that Buddhist practitioners "were less likely to be shocked, flustered, surprised, or as angry compared to other people."[5] Paul Ekman, the research leader, said: "The most reasonable hypothesis is that there is something about conscientious Buddhist practice that results in the kind of happiness we all seek."[6]

Yet all of this research, in a way, is secondary to the fact that we can each verify the value of the Buddha's teaching for ourselves, in our own life.

TAKING RESPONSIBILITY FOR HAPPINESS

To enter the path to happiness, we must first have a clear understanding of ourselves. The question "Who am I?" requires a correct answer. Our ancestors' misleading answers to this question have been crucial in preventing numerous generations from clearly seeing the path.

The Buddha identified *I* as a free individual, entirely responsible for his or her own happiness. Moreover, this *I* embodies the potential and skill to make *I* happy; no one other than oneself can make one happy. "Self-improvement or self-impairment is one's own task; someone does not improve another."[7] Even the Buddha cannot make one happy, but "only shows the path to happiness."[8]

It is essential, when preparing to achieve happiness, to first take responsibility for our own happiness. Thus self-confidence— the strong faith in our ability to make ourselves happy—plays a vital role in this initial phase.

Then, as previously discussed, we must follow the Buddha in rejecting three extremist views concerning happiness and unhappiness:

1. Our happiness and unhappiness in this present life are solely determined by the actions of our past lives.
2. Divine power solely determines our happiness or unhappiness.
3. Mere chance determines our happiness or unhappiness.[9]

Adhering to such views denies our own ability to make ourselves peaceful and content. The Buddha rejected such views. He unequivocally promoted the view that this *I* can make *I* happy: we all possess the ability, despite individual differences, to make ourselves happy.

Again, scientific research corroborates the fact that we can cultivate skills that support happiness. In late 2004, a team of researchers at the University of Wisconsin–Madison examined the brain activity of experienced meditators. Research leader Richard Davidson said of these meditators: "Their mental practice is having an effect on the brain in the same way golf or tennis practice will enhance performance."[10]

Another experiment conducted in Tibet in early 2005 with the participation of monks who practice meditation reconfirms this statement. Researchers found that "meditation can literally change the way Buddhist monks see the world."[11] They came to this conclusion after finding the monks capable of stimulating the left side of the brain, the area associated with happiness, even in the presence of unhappy visual experiences.

These experiments indicate that through the practice of meditation, in particular, we can change the structure and function of our brain. With this potential to develop our mind, we are in a position to take responsibility for our own happiness—and just a few attitudinal changes will grant us the self-confidence to do so.

BEGINNING NOW

One area that needs attention in this regard is the memory of unpleasant experiences or actions from the past. When the past continues to disturb our inner peace, happiness will continue to elude us. The Buddha advised not to allow such thoughts to disturb us: "Let the past be gone." *Now* is the right time to begin life.[12] Whatever mistakes were made in the past, they pose no hindrance if we earnestly start the search for happiness now:

> Having been negligent in the past,
> One later becomes diligent.
> That person brightens the world
> Similar to the moon emerging from behind the
>   clouds.[13]

This simile says it all: the soothing moonlight is the inner happiness we experience when we leave behind the unpleasant past. That inner brightness not only makes us happy but also allows others to be happy. And so in our effort to discover true happiness, we should first cleanse the corrupted memory. Let unpleasant memories go, determine to move ahead, and begin afresh.

The Buddha also observed that—like worries buried in the past—apprehension about the future weakens our experience of happiness. To prepare ourselves for a blissful present, we must free ourselves from such feelings. When the Buddha urged his followers to leave aside the unpleasant past, he also asked them to stop worrying about the future:

> Brooding over the future
> And repenting the past,
> The unwise wither like a green reed
> Cut down and left in the sun.[14]

This poetic expression indicates how we tend to breed sorrow while "brooding over" or fearing the future. We then suffer intensely, like an uprooted reed drying up in the sun. Appropriately, the reed mentioned here is a nala, a kind of bamboo plant that grows in shaded, watery areas. Separated from its stem and left in the sun, this reed presents a helpless and very pitiable sight. Similarly, we who unnecessarily worry about the future find it impossible to achieve inner peace.

The Buddha specifically instructed his followers that "the [unpleasant] past is dead and gone, and the future is yet to come."[15] Rumination on the unpleasant past and apprehension of the future serve no purpose to one who strives to live a happy life. Begin now, the Buddha advised, and know that this *I* can live happily if *I* begin now to follow the essential steps to happiness.

The Buddha's phrase "dwelling in happiness" does not suggest a secondary objective; it is the first and foremost objective in life. Therefore—aware that "I am dear to myself"—the wise person takes all precautionary actions for self-protection.[16]

Again, the word "protection" here means to shield against the disturbances that affect our inner peace. Who is the person who shields the mind of *I* from such disturbances? It is *I*. Constant mindfulness plays a crucial role at this juncture: constant mindfulness of the resolution to make *I* happy.

This is the advice the Buddha offered to his ordained disciples, and it will work for you as well: Be watchful while walking, standing, sitting, and lying down. And to keep your happiness undiminished, be constantly watchful for the invasive thoughts that hamper inner peace.

SEVEN STEPS TO FREEDOM FROM WORRY

Now we begin the real action, which consists of easy-to-follow techniques. Of course, like most beneficial tasks, to be free from worry requires effort. But most experienced practitioners would agree that, after shaky beginnings, their efforts succeed.

A careful study of the *Sutta Pitaka* reveals seven steps that allow us to reach this lasting form of happiness.

STEP 1: AVOID MIND-CREATED REACTIONS TO EVERYDAY EXPERIENCES

Entertaining mind-created reactions to everyday experiences was identified by the Buddha as a major obstruction to happiness.

In the *Madhupindika Sutta*, Sariputta explained this mental process clearly. By attaching our own meanings to our sensory experiences, we create unhappiness: "One reproduces and enlarges what one reasons about," he remarked. "As a result, one allows such thoughts to attack oneself."[17]

This sutta explains a deep but ordinary psychological process that keeps our inner peace at bay. Human nature urges us to interpret sensory experiences, but our interpretations often depend on assumptions, not on facts. The Pali word for this so-called interpretation is *papanceti*, which means to "grow within" or "enlarge in the mind"—a psychological process that tends to hurt rather than benefit us. Thus thoughts that "attack oneself" refer to this inner disturbance.

For example: "He didn't smile because he doesn't like me." The claim is an actual visual experience; the reasoning that supports it is clearly a mental one—and the instant aftermath is unhappiness. Being watchful, we can observe how quickly our happy mood turns around when negative assumptions interfere.

Worst of all, the mind does not stop there; it continues to create more "why" questions and "because" answers. "Why doesn't he like me?" one might ask next. And the instant answer might be "Because he thinks I am stupid." This process goes on and on, only worsening the misery that has already settled in the mind.

Of course, assumptions are important for finding the right answers to questions. According to the Buddha's teaching, however, the belief that assumptions are true will neither lead us to right answers nor make us happy. In the previous example, the actual reason why "he didn't smile" may be altogether different. Someone in a thoughtful mood may miss visual objects; in an unhappy mood, he or she may fail to be cheerful. This may have been why the person did not smile. His cheerful appearance the next day would convince me I was mistaken—but the unhappiness caused by misjudgments will have already taken its toll.

Sariputta explained that we attach meanings to our experiences and consequently create unhappy moods, even when objects are not present to our senses. Depending on past experiences stored in memory, we create imaginary pictures that only drag us into unhappy territory. "Thoughts [also] arise as a result of mind and [mere] mental objects," remarked Sariputta, regarding the connection between senses and sensual objects.[18] These thoughts also go through a process of evaluation and eventually influence our mood in a negative way.

We may look into ourselves to find out how true this statement is. On a peaceful day, we may suddenly find ourselves trapped by an unhappy thought coming out of nowhere. These thoughts occur as we mentally retrieve our past experiences and reevaluate the unpleasant meanings attached to those experiences. Consequently, we deprive ourselves of the inner peace with which we began the day. In reality, however, neither these experiences nor their meanings exist anywhere other than in our minds. How irrational it is to let a nonexistent experience destroy happiness, the most precious thing in our life!

The Buddha's teaching encourages us to refrain from clinging to self-created meanings given to sensual objects. Especially, as we recognize a sound or a sight or remember a similar experience in the past, we should see it as it is, not as something to be expanded with self-invented causes. This practice will contribute immensely to the happiness we are all looking for.

STEP 2: LET GO OF GREED AND MALICE

We have already discussed greed and malicious thoughts in detail, but we return to this topic to highlight its relationship to happiness. The Buddha saw nothing more detrimental to happiness than these two forms of mental reaction. "Greed breeds unhappiness; greed breeds fear," he said. "When greed ceases to exist, no unhappiness or fear exists."[19] Referring to malice, he mentioned that those who eliminate it "live happily and peacefully among the haters."[20] In the *Sutta Pitaka* the Buddha constantly repeated that absence of greed and malice in the mind makes us exceedingly happy.

Still, people fail, or rather do not make a serious effort, to have control over greed and malicious thoughts in real life. They give way to these two natural urges repeatedly. The human mind, according to the Buddha, is basically brilliant, but becomes polluted as a result of its contact with the external world.[21] Nothing does more to pollute the human mind and cloud its natural happiness than greed and malice.

Awareness of mind's tendencies is the first step in achieving peace of mind. "When a lustful thought occurs, one should know that it is a lustful thought," the Buddha instructed.[22] Similarly, we need to be vigilant about other thoughts, feelings, and emotions that occur in our minds.[23]

The main reason most of us fail to curb greed and malicious thought is an inability to recognize their presence in our minds. Driven by these urges, we unknowingly allow our feelings and emotions to control us. By contrast, when we detect the presence of unwholesome thoughts within, we know what to do next.

Without a genuine effort, we may allow our inner feelings to take a firm grip on ourselves instead of managing to take hold of the feeling itself. However, those who make a purposeful attempt succeed in their effort and take a giant step forward: they prevent themselves from being taken into an unhappy state. They understand that the departure from burning desire and anger-dominated thoughts is soothing indeed for the mind.

STEP 3: PURSUE A GOAL AND ENJOY ACHIEVING IT

While the Buddha identified a greedy action as a forerunner of inner suffering, he recognized pursuit of a goal and the consequent achievement of it as a clear basis for individual happiness. The term *atthi sukha* indicates this source of happiness. As it was defined in the *Anguttara Nikaya*, *atthi sukha* suggests the happy thoughts derived from achieving material success through just means. In a broader sense, any form of success achieved through rightful means is a source of happiness, according to the Buddha.

To understand the difference between a greed-motivated action and a goal, we need to evaluate both in terms of their objectives. In basic terms, a greedy action disregards the well-being of others while overemphasizing one's own sensory satisfaction. A goal, in contrast, relies on one's own potential, and its achievement brings benefits for oneself and others. The Buddha clearly stressed that such an achievement does make us happy.

We may look at the Buddha's own life to understand the truth of this statement. For seven years he strove to attain enlightenment, the most noteworthy objective in his life. After a strenuous endeavor that symbolized the fruitfulness of human effort, he eventually attained his objective. What did he do immediately afterward? For three weeks he remained in solitude and enjoyed his remarkable achievement. He derived great happiness from thinking about what many people dreamed about, but that only he had attained.

Again, in a teaching given in his later years, the Buddha looked back to contemplate another achievement that gave him immense satisfaction. He reviewed the remarkable feat he had achieved during the forty-five years since his enlightenment:

> I am now old.... I have come to the end of my journey. Yet, I have senior, experienced, skillful...bhikkhus, laymen, and laywomen. This society is successful, prosperous, widespread, and popular.... I don't see any teacher who has reached such a renowned position as I am in.[24]

What the Buddha achieved between his enlightenment and his death may be one of the greatest achievements by a single human being during one lifetime. Not only did he establish a progressive new society within the traditional, rigid Vedic society, he also convinced most traditionalists to abandon their beliefs and practices and to join him. He profoundly influenced people's ways of thinking and brought about drastic social changes. The quotation cited above shows his rightful appreciation of his great achievement. He happily visualized what he had begun in his mid-thirties, and then achieved several decades later.

Obviously, the word "achievement" does not mean the completion of a gigantic task that only a sprinkling of people would be capable of. From the Buddha's point of view, "achievement" means any accomplishment associated with either inner development or social success. Most of the Buddha's ordained disciples regarded their spiritual development—their ability to handle greed, malice, and illusion—as their highest achievement. This accomplishment gave them a stable form of happiness throughout their lives. The members of his lay community also obtained a similar form of happiness by thinking over their own meaningful lives, which, from the Buddha's point of view, was a notable achievement.

Specifically for the lay community, the Buddha stated that financial success is an achievement that would bring happiness upon reflection. As already discussed, *atthi sukha* means "the happiness derived from thinking over the achievements in the field of money and wealth." This achievement may include not only the wealth one has accumulated with right effort but also the knowledge and skill one developed in order to gain financial strength. An educational qualification that would enhance one's financial stability, for instance, belongs to this category. One may think of the milestones on one's way to financial strength as a source of happiness.

We observe that reflection upon a greed-driven action done in the past would hardly make us happy, while visualization of an achievement would rarely fail to please us. A greedy action—overindulgence in sensory satisfaction, for instance—is gone, and an effort to refresh the mind with such an action would yield only an uneasy emptiness. The achievement of a worthwhile goal remains with us and becomes a source of enjoyment.

STEP 4: LOOK AT OTHERS' UNPLEASANT ACTIONS WITH COMPASSION

The Buddha also maintained that our own compassionate attitude toward people who exhibit some noisome behavior would help us stabilize our own inner peace. When the destructive urge slowly leaves us, two notable changes take place inside. First, anger, hatred, and other related feelings and emotions lose their grip within us. Next, the mind opens its gates for compassionate feelings to pour in. We realize that the people who previously appeared so noisome to us now deserve our compassion. This realization further strengthens our inner peace.

This statement does not suggest that those who commit inhuman actions should be tolerated, and that the related consequences should be ignored. Clearly, the Buddha endeavored throughout his life to change human actions that caused unwholesome consequences. Such topics as social discrimination and violence never escaped his attention. He argued assertively and convincingly against such practices, and successfully launched a huge campaign in order to change them. The Buddha never advocated tolerance of harmful human behavior as a way to keep our mind at peace.

However, we observe that what destroys our inner peace on a daily basis is most often not crime, corruption, and malpractice in society, but the simple experiences in our day-to-day life. A speeding driver cutting into our lane, a coworker rarely having a happy face, or a roommate failing to wash the dishes may disturb us more than a heinous crime in the city would. Of course, people should improve, and their unpleasant behavior should change, however trivial it appears to be. Yet, taking these relatively trivial actions into our own hearts would only ruin the happiness that we are all entitled to.

Therefore, following the Buddha's advice, we rightly view the actions of those people compassionately instead of allowing them to destroy our own happiness. The most effective way to understand some people's unusually annoying behavior and, consequently, to feel compassion toward them is to see them as imperfect human beings, just as we all are. The Buddha pointed out that "mental imbalance" is one of the most notable occurrences among human beings. Every individual, according to his explanation, possesses some anomaly. Unawareness of this fact leads us to make a big mistake when we interpret some noisome human behavior: we believe that such behavior is deliberate and intentional.

Of course, others must train themselves to behave well—and the Buddha asserted that they can—but their failure to do so should not be allowed to rob us of our own peace of mind. This approach clearly protects our own peace of mind.

Practicing loving-kindness meditation seems to be a very effective habit for this purpose. Right understanding almost always gives rise to compassion. We understand that no reaction would be more appropriate than feeling compassion toward those who exhibit unpleasant behavior. So, we focus on those people and repeat to ourselves, "May you be well, happy, and peaceful!"

Nobody can guarantee that we can change others and make them happy. Yet, we should know that we possess enormous power to improve ourselves and make ourselves happy. The Buddha summed up this attitude poetically:

> We live so happily
> Among the people with inner difficulties.
> We live as healthy ones
> Among disturbed people.[25]

STEP 5: WORK FOR OTHERS' BENEFIT

The Buddha clearly identified as myth a belief that people still hold to be a profound truth: the more we satisfy our own senses, the happier we will be. He actually discovered the opposite to be true. Those who fulfill their duties toward others, who alleviate the suffering of others, and who contribute to social progress are actually the happy people.

As previously discussed, several of the Buddha's contemporaries promoted the erroneous view that indulgence in sensory satisfaction would make people happy. Some of these "teachers" blatantly disregarded social ethics. They claimed that sensory satisfaction would be identical with happiness, but the Buddha's key phrase *bhoga sukha* ("happiness gained through the usage of wealth") clarifies his opposition to this mistaken view. From his viewpoint, one can achieve happiness by using one's wealth not only for oneself but also for others.

According to this clarification, we can derive great satisfaction by fulfilling our duties to parents, children, friends, and others. Of course, the Buddha reminded us that we should not neglect our own well-being, but that attention to others' well-being is a great source of happiness.

Parents can be happy because they have guided their children to the highest possible level. Adult children can be happy because they have fulfilled their obligations toward their aging parents. We are all happy because we have helped the needy, participated in volunteer work, or donated to a meaningful cause. What we do for others makes us genuinely happy.

The Buddha observed that both *bhavana* and *dana* are great practices that lead us toward happiness. As discussed in the previous chapter, *bhavana* means "inner development," for which cultivation of compassion is a basic requirement. When compassion grows in the mind, happiness also shines. *Dana* (the practice of generosity) is the external manifestation of compassion developed internally. If we are compassionate, we, undoubtedly, practice generosity. That practice also leads us to happiness, similar to what compassion does.

STEP 6: LIVE A PRINCIPLED LIFE

The Buddha further elaborated that a principled life would grant us a great opportunity to find peace within ourselves. He used the term *anavajja sukha* to mean this important source of inner peace. On several occasions, the Buddha remarked that we do not have to wait for the next life to receive the positive effects of our wholesome actions. By practicing uprightness, we can find inner peace in our present life. The Pali sentence *kathapunno idha nandati* epitomizes this teaching. *Kathapunno* is the person who lives a life full of principles and values, and such a person finds happiness in this very life (*idha nandati*).

Two questions await explanation at this point. First, what are the characteristics of the "person who lives a life full of principles"? Next, how does such a person achieve happiness?

We have three Pali words—*punna, kusala,* and *dhamma*—that convey basically the same meaning: disciplined and upright way of living. Throughout his life, the Buddha strove to lead people to *punna, kusala,* or *dhamma* and to prevent them from practicing their opposites: *papa, akusala,* or *adhamma.* The following words, spoken by one of the Buddha's disciples, convey his advice on living a principled life:

> Avoidance of unwholesome actions,
> Practice of wholesome actions,
> Development of mind:
> This is what the Buddha insists on.[26]

Principled life, then, means a combination of upright conduct and wholesome thought. With right evaluation, we refrain
from doing unwholesome actions and speaking unwholesome
words. We also carefully select the right actions and the right
words. To match the modification of our external behavior, we
strive to develop our thoughts. This effort characterizes principled life.

Living such a life seems to connect to individual happiness
more closely than one might expect. In fact, such actions provide a soothing experience to our mind. "A layperson lives his
or her life with righteous words, righteous deeds, and righteous thoughts. By thinking about the righteous way of living,
he or she derives happiness and inner peace," the Buddha
explained.27 Perhaps righteous acts do not bring their fullest
effects immediately, but in the long run their positive effects on
our mental health become more manifest.

The Buddha further clarified that an intentional deed takes
time to mature in our minds. The word he used was *paccati.* The
terms *punnam paccati* and *papam paccati* mean that both wholesome and unwholesome actions gather momentum in the mind
as time goes by. "When unwholesome actions done in the past
gradually mature internally, the person experiences more
unhappiness," the Buddha said.28 In contrast, a matured wholesome action makes the person exceedingly happy.

Maturation suggests development and firm establishment of
such actions within ourselves. As we reflect on these actions,
they grow and find a permanent place within us. While
unpleasant actions begin to haunt us, wholesome actions continue to soothe us. Most people find that qualities such as their
own truthfulness, generosity, and nonviolence pave the way for
them to achieve peace of mind. Thus, our own noble principles
grant us a dependable source of happiness.

STEP 7. ACCEPT THE INEVITABILITY OF CHANGE AS NATURAL LAW

The Buddha emphasized human potential as a greatly effective factor in bringing about positive changes to human life. He stated that we do possess the ability to change the physical world and to improve the quality of life. His advice to King Kosala, that controlled eating grants one a long and healthy life,[29] is just one example. However, the Buddha did not present a totalizing theory. We cannot change everything, particularly the natural process of human life. Inner peace, he explained, is attainable not by denying natural laws but by accepting them as inseparable from life.

At the very core of the Buddha's philosophy is the teaching of impermanence, or *anicca*. "All physical phenomenon is subject to change."[30] Realization of this truth is crucial to remaining unperturbed by various natural occurrences in life. The Buddha said, "One who realizes the impermanence of all natural phenomena finds inner peace."[31]

Such conditions as disease, physical deterioration, death, and separation from loved ones, according to the Buddha's classification, are a part of natural law. Of course, we can minimize or postpone these occurrences in our lives, but we can never stop them. Development of wisdom to accept these inevitable changes calmly is the only rational approach.

The Buddha specifically encouraged his lay followers to see themselves as a part of nature, instead of regarding their bodies as objects of attachment. Developed as a form of meditation, this attitude brings realization and acceptance of the inevitability of physical change.

He never advised his disciples to develop a pessimistic attitude toward life. Amid such unavoidable conditions as sickness and physical deterioration, he paved the way for their inner peace and happiness.

Thoughts and actions of compassion, generosity, dutifulness, and upright conduct are outstanding practices to soothe our minds. And the wisdom to accept inevitable change makes our inner peace and happiness lasting and complete. This truly is a teaching that "is excellent at the beginning, excellent in the middle, excellent in the end."[32]

Epigraph taken from: *Anguttara Nikaya III*: Puggala Vagga: Andha Sutta and *Anguttara Nikaya X*: Akankha Vagga: Vaddhi Sutta

    Note: The epigraph combines two separate sources. The Buddha defined the wise layperson in the Andha Sutta and talked about his lay followers' tenfold development in the Vaddhi Sutta.

CHAPTER 1

Epigraph taken from: *Anguttara Nikaya III*: Bharandu Vagga: Paticchanna Sutta

1. *Samyutta Nikaya I*: Kosala Samyutta: Pancaraja Sutta; *The Connected Discourses of the Buddha*: 175–176

2. *Anguttara Nikaya II*: Sukha Vagga: 1–2; *The Connected Discourses of the Buddha*: 1283–1285

3. *Samyutta Nikaya IV*: Vedana Samyutta: Niramisa Sutta

    Note: The term *samisa piti* has been translated as "happiness in worldly life." *Samisa* means "carnal" or "belonging to secular life." In this sutta, the Buddha repeats the same adjectives to describe sound, smell, taste, and physical contact. The translation avoids the repetitions.

4. *Samyutta Nikaya XI*: Sotapatti Samyutta: Veludvareyya Sutta; *The Connected Discourses of the Buddha*: 1796–1799

CHAPTER 2

Epigraph taken from: *Anguttara Nikaya VI*: Dhammika Vagga: Ina Sutta

1. *Anguttara Nikaya VIII*: Gotami Vagga: Vyagghapajja Sutta

2. *Samyutta Nikaya I*: Kosala Samyutta: Pathama Aputtaka Sutta; *The Connected Discourses of the Buddha*: 182–183

3. *Anguttara Nikaya IV*: Pattakamma Vagga: Anana Sutta

4. *Digha Nikaya I*: 2: Samannaphala Sutta; *The Long Discourses of the Buddha*: 125–136

5. Ibid.
6. *Digha Nikaya III*: 31: Sigalovada Sutta; *The Long Discourses of the Buddha*: 461–469
7. *Anguttara Nikaya VIII*: Yamaka Vagga: Dutiya Sampada Sutta
8. *Digha Nikaya III*: 31: Sigalovada Sutta; *The Long Discourses of the Buddha*: 461–469
9. *Anguttara Nikaya V*: Mundaraja Vagga: Pancabhoga Adiya Sutta
   Note: The word *atithi* is generally translated as "visitors," but this translation is incorrect. The Buddha, in this quotation, has already mentioned relatives, friends, and associates. One finds no other "visitors" to one's house. The correct translation seems to be "the needy"—those who visit a house to request food or other necessities.
10. *Samyutta Nikaya I*: Kosala Samyutta: Pathama Aputtaka Sutta; *The Connected Discourses of the Buddha*: 182–183
11. *Anguttara Nikaya V*: Mundaraja Vagga: Sappurisa Sutta
12. *Digha Nikaya III*: 31: Sigalovada Sutta; *The Long Discourses of the Buddha*: 461–469
13. Ibid.
14. *Sutta Nipata*: Uraga Vagga
15. *Samyutta Nikaya I*: Kosala Samyutta: Appaka Sutta; *The Connected Discourses of the Buddha*: 169–170
16. Ibid.
17. *Samyutta Nikaya I*: Kosala Samyutta: Donapaka Sutta; *The Connected Discourses of the Buddha*: 176–177

CHAPTER 3

Epigraph taken from: *Anguttara Nikaya II*: Sotapatti Samyutta: Upannasa Sutta and *Anguttara Nikaya VIII*: Gotami Vagga: Vyagghapajja Sutta
   Note: This epigraph combines the two sources given above. The first sentence of the epigraph is from Upannasa Sutta. Referring to his own enlightenment, The Buddha made this statement in order to emphasize the motivation for achievement. The original Pali term *asantutthita kusalesu dhammesu* has been translated as "not to be content with what I have achieved." The phrase *kusalesu dhammesu* defies any direct translation. In context, this phrase means the Buddha's achievements in his inner development, excluding the final achievement of enlightenment.
1. *Anguttara Nikaya III*: Maha Vagga: Titthayatana Sutta

2. Ibid.

3. Ibid.

4. *Anguttara Nikaya II:* Vassupanayika Vagga: Uposatha Sutta

5. *Anguttara Nikaya VIII:* Gotami Vagga: Vyagghapajja Sutta

6. *Anguttara Nikaya III:* Rathakara Vagga: Dutiya Papanika Sutta

7. *Digha Nikaya III:* 31; *The Long Discourses of the Buddha:* 461–469

8. *Sutta Nipata:* Culla Vagga: Mangala Sutta

9. *Sumangala Vilasini:* Brahmajala Sutta Vannana

10. *Sutta Nipata:* Uraga Vagga: Parabhava Sutta

11. *Digha Nikaya III:* 31: Sigalovada Sutta; *The Long Discourses of the Buddha:* 461–469

12. *Anguttara Nikaya VIII:* Uposatha Vagga: Anuruddha Manapakayika Sutta

13. *Samyutta Nikaya I:* Kosala Samyutta: Appamada Sutta; *The Connected Discourses of the Buddha:* 179–180

14. *Digha Nikaya III:* 31: Sigalovada Sutta; *The Long Discourses of the Buddha:* 461–469

15. Ibid.

16. *Samyutta Nikaya I:* Kosala Samyutta: Kalyanamitta Sutta; *The Connected Discourses of the Buddha:* 180–182

17. Ibid.

18. *Dhammapada:* Verse 155

19. *Digha Nikaya III:* 31: Sigalovada Sutta; *The Long Discourses of the Buddha:* 461–469

CHAPTER 4

Epigraph taken from: *Anguttara Nikaya IV:* Pattakamma Vagga: Pattakamma Sutta

Note: The Pali phrase *dullabho* (*du*="difficult"+*labho*="to obtain") has been translated as "achievable through effort." Taken with the positive adjectives "pleasant," "agreeable," and "charming," the adjective *dullabho* should convey a positive connotation.

1. *Anguttara Nikaya IV:* Abhinna Vagga: Kula Sutta

2. *Anguttara Nikaya IV:* Pattakamma Vagga: Pattakamma Sutta

3. Ibid.

4. *Anguttara Nikaya IV:* Pattakamma Vagga: Pattakamma Sutta

5. Ibid.

6. Ibid.

7. *Anguttara Nikaya VIII:* Gotami Vagga: Vyagghapajja Sutta

8. *Digha Nikaya III:* 31: Sigalovada Sutta; *The Long Discourses of the Buddha:* 461–469

9. *Samyutta Nikaya I:* Kosala Samyutta: Sattajatila Sutta; *The Connected Discourses of the Buddha:* 173–174

10. *Digha Nikaya III:* 31: Sigalovada Sutta; *The Long Discourses of the Buddha:* 461–469

11. Ibid.

12. Ibid.

13. Ibid.

14. Ibid.

15. *Anguttara Nikaya VIII:* Gotami Vagga: Vyagghapajja Sutta

16. *Anguttara Nikaya IV:* Pattakamma Vagga: Anana Sutta

17. *Anguttara Nikaya VIII:* Gotami Vagga: Vyagghapajja Sutta

18. *Anguttata Nikaya IV:* Pattakamma Vagga: Pattakamma Sutta

19. Ibid.

20. Ibid.

21. *Sutta Nipata:* Culla Vagga: Mangala Sutta

22. *Dhammapada:* Verse 47

23. *Anguttara Nikaya III:* Bala Vagga: Bhaya Sutta

24. *Digha Nikaya III:* 31: Sigalovada Sutta; *The Long Discourses of the Buddha:* 461–465

25. Ibid.

26. *Samyutta Nikaya I:* Kosala Samyutta: Kalyanamitta Sutta; *The Connected Discourses of the Buddha:* 180–182

27. *Anguttara Nikaya VIII:* Gotami Vagga: Ujjaya Sutta

28. *Sutta Nipata:* Uraga Vagga: Parabhava Sutta

29. *Digha Nikaya III:* 31: Sigalovada Sutta; *The Long Discourses of the Buddha:* 461–469

30. Ibid.

31. *Anguttara Nikaya VIII:* Gotami Vagga: Vyagghapajja Sutta

32. *Digha Nikaya III:* 31: Sigalovada Sutta; *The Long Discourses of the Buddha:* 461–469

33. Ibid.

34. Ibid.

CHAPTER 5

Epigraph taken from: *Samyutta Nikaya I:* Kosala Samyutta: Sattajatila Sutta; *The Connected Discourses of the Buddha:* 173–174

1. *Sutta Nipata:* Uraga Vagga: Khaggavisana Sutta
2. *Samyutta Nikaya I:* Brahmana Samyutta: Sundarika Sutta; *The Connected Discourses of the Buddha:* 262–263
3. *Anguttara Nikaya I:* Bala Vagga
4. *Sutta Nipata:* Uraga Vagga: Vasala Sutta
5. *Anguttara Nikaya VIII:* Gotami Vagga: Gotami Sutta
6. *Samyutta Nikaya I:* Kosala Samyutta: Sattajatila Sutta; *The Connected Discourses of the Buddha:* 173–174
7. Ibid.
8. Ibid.
9. *Anguttara Nikaya III:* Bala Vagga: Bhaya Sutta
10. *Anguttara Nikaya IV:* Punnabhisanda Vagga: Pathama Samajiva Sutta

CHAPTER 6

Epigraph taken from: *Anguttara Nikaya IV:* Punnabhisanda Vagga: Pathama Samvasa Sutta

1. *Anguttara Nikaya IV:* Punnabhisanda Vagga: Pathama Samvasa Sutta
2. *Digha Nikaya III:* 31: Sigalovada Sutta; *The Long Discourses of the Buddha:* 461–469
3. Ibid.
4. *Samyutta Nikaya V:* Sotapatti Samyutta: Veludvareyya Sutta; *The Connected Discourses of the Buddha:* 1796–1799
5. *Anguttara Nikaya I:* Ekaka Vagga
6. *Anguttara Nikaya VII:* Avyakata Vagga: Sattabhariya Sutta
7. *Digha Nikaya III:* 31: Sigalovada Sutta; *The Long Discourses of the Buddha:* 461–469
8. Ibid.
9. *Anguttara Nikaya VIII:* Gotami Vagga: Gotami Sutta
10. *Anguttara Nikaya VIII:* Uposatha Vagga: Nakulamatumanapakayika Sutta
11. *Digha Nikaya III:* 31: Sigalovada Sutta; *The Long Discourses of the Buddha:* 461–469
12. *Anguttara Nikaya VII:* Avyakata Vagga: Sattabhariya Sutta
13. Ibid.

CHAPTER 7

Epigraph taken from: *Anguttara Nikaya III:* Devaduta Vagga: Sabrahmaka Sutta

1. *Anguttara Nikaya VIII:* Gotami Vagga: Vyagghapajja Sutta

2. *Samyutta Nikaya I:* Brahmana Samyutta: Mahasala Sutta; *The Connected Discourses of the Buddha:* 271–272
3. *Samyutta Nikaya I:* Kosala Samyutta: Pathama Aputtaka Sutta; *The Connected Discourses of the Buddha:* 182–183
4. *Sutta Nipata:* Culla Vagga
5. *Digha Nikaya III:* 31: Sigalovada Sutta; *The Long Discourses of the Buddha:* 461–469
6. *Dhammapada:* Verse 129
7. *Dhammapada:* Verse 133
8. *Dhammapada:* Verse 158
9. *Digha Nikaya III:* 31: Sigalovada Sutta; *The Long Discourses of the Buddha:* 461–469
10. *Majjhima Nikaya II:* 58: Abhaya Rajakumara Sutta; *The Middle Length Discourses of the Buddha:* 498–501
11. *Majjhima Nikaya II:* 61: Ambalatthika Rahulovada Sutta; *The Middle Length Discourses of the Buddha:* 523–526
12. *Sutta Nipata:* Culla Vagga

CHAPTER 8

Epigraph taken from: *Anguttara Nikaya V:* Aghata Vagga: Codana Sutta
1. *Anguttara Nikaya V:* Sona Vagga: Subhasitavaca Sutta; *Anguttara Nikaya V:* Agatha Vagga: Codana Sutta
2. *Majjhima Nikaya I:* 27: Culahatthipadopama Sutta; *The Middle Length Discourses of the Buddha:* 269–277
3. *Anguttara Nikaya V:* Raja Vagga: Pathama Cakkanuvattana Sutta
4. *Dhammapadatthakatha:* Sahassa Vagga: Kisagotamiya Vatthu
5. *Dhammapadatthakatha:* Sukha Vagggga: Annatarassa Upasakassa Vatthu
6. *Dhammapadatthakatha:* Citta Vagga: Putigattatissatthera Vatthu
7. *Anguttara Nikaya V:* Aghata Vagga: Codana Sutta
8. *Majjhima Nikaya II:* 58: Abhayarajakumara Sutta; *The Middle Length Discourses of the Buddha:* 498–501
9. Verse 232
10. *Sutta Nipata:* Cula Vagga: Hiri Sutta
11. *Anguttara Nikaya V:* Aghata Vagga: Codana Sutta
12. Ibid.
13. *Digha Nikaya I:* 8: Maha Sihanada Sutta; *The Long Discourses of the Buddha:* 151–157
14. *Anguttara Nikaya IV:* Indriya Vagga: Roga Sutta

15. *Anguttara Nikaya III:* Bala Vagga: Accaya Sutta
16. *Anguttara Nikaya III:* Puggala Vagga: Vajiropama Sutta
17. *Majjhima Nikaya II:* 86: Angulimala Sutta; *The Middle Length Discourses of the Buddha:* 710–717
18. *Anguttara Nikaya I:* Ekaka Vagga: 1
19. *Anguttara Nikaya I:* Ekaka Vagga: 2
20. *Anguttara Nikaya III:* Bala Vagga: Accaya Sutta
21. *Dhammapada:* Verse 329
22. *Majjhima Nikaya II:* 56: Upali Sutta; *The Middle Length Discourses of the Buddha:* 477–492
23. *Anguttara Nikaya VIII:* Gahapati Vagga: Hatthigamaka Ugga Sutta
24. *Anguttara Nikaya IV:* Kesi Vagga: Kesi Sutta
25. *Dhammapada:* Verse 3

CHAPTER 9

Epigraph taken from: *Digha Nikaya I:* 4: Sonadanda Sutta; *The Long Discourses of the Buddha:* 125–132
1. *Majjhima Nikaya II:* 96: Esukari Sutta; *The Middle Length Discourses of the Buddha:* 789–790
2. *Udana:* Sona Vagga: Uposatha Sutta
3. *Anguttara Nikaya VIII:* Gotami Samyutta: Gotami Sutta
   Note: At the beginning of this conversation, the Buddha's reluctance to permit the ordination of women is mostly due to social factors. An ordained disciple of the Buddha had to practice meditation in solitude, often in a forest or in an empty house. In that society, such places were extremely dangerous for women. Apparently, the Buddha did not want to cause problems for women by offering them ordination. However, after listening to Ananda's rational argument, the Buddha agreed to offer ordination to women.
4. *Samyutta Nikaya V:* Bhikkhuni Samyutta: Soma Sutta; *The Connected Discourses of the Buddha:* 222–223
5. *Sutta Nipata:* Uraga Vagga: Vasala Sutta
6. *Majjhima Nikaya II:* 96: Esukari Sutta; *The Middle Length Discourses of the Buddha:* 789–790
7. *Anguttara Nikaya X:* Maha Vagga: Dutiya Mahapanna Sutta
8. *Majjhima Nikaya II:* 72: Aggivacchagotta Sutta; *The Middle Length Discourses of the Buddha:* 590–594
9. *Digha Nikaya III:* 27: Aggañña Sutta; *The Long Discourses of the Buddha:* 407–415

10. Ibid.

11. *Majjhima Nikaya II:* 72: Aggivacchagotta Sutta; *The Middle Length Discourses of the Buddha:* 590–594

12. *Sutta Nipata:* Atthaka Vagga: Pasura Sutta

13. *Majjhima Nikaya II:* 58: Abhayarajakumara Sutta; *The Middle Length Discourses of the Buddha:* 498–501

14. *Majjhima Nikaya II:* 79: Culasakuludayi Sutta; *The Middle Length Discourses of the Buddha:* 654–662

15. *Digha Nikaya I:* 8: Mahasihanada Sutta; *The Long Discourses of the Buddha:* 151–157

CHAPTER 10

Epigraph taken from: *Anguttara Nikaya I:* Ekadhamma Pali: Dutiya Vagga: 3–4

1. *Majjhima Nikaya II:* 95: Canki Sutta; *The Middle Length Discourses of the Buddha:* 775–785

2. Ibid.

3. *Majjhima Nikaya II:* 76: Sandaka Sutta; *The Middle Length Discourses of the Buddha:* 618–628

4. *Digha Nikaya I:* 13: Tevijja Sutta; *The Long Discourses of the Buddha:* 187–195

5. *Digha Nikaya III:* 31: Sigalovada Sutta; *The Long Discourses of the Buddha:* 461–469

6. *Digha Nikaya III:* 27: Agganna Sutta; *The Long Discourses of the Buddha:* 407–415

7. Ibid.

8. *Majjhima Nikaya II:* 84: Madhura Sutta; *The Middle Length Discourses of the Buddha:* 698–703

9. *Digha Nikaya III:* 27: Agganna Sutta; *The Middle Length Discourses of the Buddha:* 407–415

10. *Digha Nikaya I:* 2: Samannaphala Sutta; *The Long Discourses of the Buddha:* 91–109

11. *Samyutta Nikaya I:* Kosala Samyutta: Sattajatila Sutta; *The Connected Discourses of the Buddha:* 173–174

12. *Digha Nikaya I:* 4: Sonadanda Sutta; *The Long Discourses of the Buddha:* 125–132

13. *Digha Nikaya I:* 11: Kevaddha Sutta; *The Long Discourses of the Buddha:* 175–180

14. *Majjhima Nikaya II:* 76: Sandaka Sutta; *The Middle Length Discourses of the Buddha:* 618–628

15. *Digha Nikaya III:* 27; *The Long Discourses of the Buddha:* 407–415
16. Ibid.
17. *Digha Nikaya I:* 3: Ambattha Sutta; *The Long Discourses of the Buddha:* 111–124
18. Ibid.
19. *Majjhima Nikaya II:* 92: Sela Sutta; *The Middle Length Discourses of the Buddha:* 755–762
20. Ibid.
21. *Majjhima Nikaya I:* 35: Culasaccaka Sutta; *The Middle Length Discourses of the Buddha:*
22. *Majjhima Nikaya II:* 56: Upali Sutta; *The Middle Length Discourses of the Buddha:* 477–492
23. *Majjhima Nikaya II:* 95: Canki Sutta; *The Middle Length Discourses of the Buddha:* 775–785
24. Ibid.
25. Ibid.
26. Ibid.

CHAPTER 11

Epigraph taken from: *Anguttara Nikaya III:* Maha Vagga: Kalama Sutta
1. *Digha Nikaya I:* 13: Tevijja Sutta; *The Long Discourses of the Buddha:* 187–195
2. *Anguttara Nikaya III:* Maha Vagga: Kalama Sutta
3. *Digha Nikaya I:* 13: Tevijja Sutta; *The Long Discourses of the Buddha:* 187–195
4. *Majjhima Nikaya II:* 98: Vasettha Sutta; *The Middle Length Discourses of the Buddha:* 798–808
5. *Anguttara Nikaya I:* Pamada Vagga: 5; *The Middle Length Discourses of the Buddha:* 677–691
6. *Dhammapada:* Verse 216
7. *Anguttara Nikaya III:* Ananda Vagga: Ananda Sutta
8. *Anguttara Nikaya III:* Maha Vagga: Akusalamula Sutta
9. *Anguttara Nikaya III:* Ananda Vagga: Ananda Sutta
10. *Dhammapada:* Verse 5
11. *Dhammapadatthakatha:* 1. 4: Kaliyakkhiniya Uppatti Vatthu
12. *Dhammapadatthakatha:* 15. 1: Kalahavupasamana Vatthu
13. *Anguttara Nikaya VII:* Abyakata Vagga: Kodhana Sutta
14. *Angutara Nikaya III:* Maha Vagga: Akusalamula Sutta
15. *Anguttara Nikaya III:* Ananda Vagga: Ananda Sutta
16. *Majjhima Nikaya II:* 82: Ratthapala Sutta; *The Middle Length Discourses of the Buddha:* 677–691

17. *Anguttara Nikaya III:* Ananda Vagga: Ananda Sutta
18. *Anguttara Nikaya III:* Maha Vagga: Akusalamula Sutta
19. *Anguttara Nikaya III:* Ananda Vagga: Ananda Sutta
20. *Majjhima Nikaya II:* 61: Ambalatthikarahulovada Sutta; *The Middle Length Discourses of the Buddha:* 523–526
21. *Anguttara Nikaya III:* Maha Vagga: Kalama Sutta

CHAPTER 12

Epigraph taken from: *Sutta Nipata:* Culla Vagga: Mangala Sutta
1. *Samyutta Nikaya V:* Sotapatti Samyutta: Veludvareyya Sutta; *The Connected Discourses of the Buddha:* 1796–1799
2. *Dhammapada:* Verse 182
3. *Vimanavatthu Atthakatha:* Rajjumala Vimana
4. *Anguttara Nikaya VII:* Avyakata Vagga: Kodhana Sutta
5. *Majjhima Nikaya III:* 144: Channovada Sutta; *The Middle Length Discourses of the Buddha:* 1114–1116; *Samyutta Nikaya III:* Khandha Samyutta: Vakkali Sutta; *The Connected Discourses of the Buddha:* 938–941
6. *Dhammapada:* Verse 131
7. *Digha Nikaya I:* 5; *The Long Discourses of the Buddha:* 133–141
8. *Anguttara Nikaya V:* Upasaka Vagga: Gihi Sutta
9. *Samyutta Nikaya V:* Sotapatti Samyutta: Veludvareyya Sutta; *The Connected Discourses of the Buddha:* 1796–1799
10. *Anguttara Nikaya I:* Cittapariyadana Vagga
11. *Anguttara Nikaya VIII:* Uposatha Vagga: Dutiyavisakha Sutta
12. *Samyutta Nikaya V:* Sotapatti Samyutta: Veludvareyya Sutta; *The Connected Discourses of the Buddha:* 1796–1799
13. *Majjima Nikaya I:* 41: Saleyyaka Sutta; *The Middle Length Discourses of the Buddha:* 379–385
14. *Digha Nikaya II:* 16: Mahaparinibbana Sutta; *The Long Discourses of the Buddha:* 231–277
15. *Samyutta Nikaya IV:* Gamini Samyutta: Pataliya Sutta; *The Connected Discourses of the Buddha:* 1361–1362
    Note: The Pali sentence *Ayam puriso… kulitthisu kulakumarisu carittam apajji* (This man got himself into sexual activity with protected women and girls) suggests forced sex.
16. *Anguttara Nikaya V:* Nivarana Vagga: Mataputta Sutta
17. *Digha Nikaya III:* 26: Cakkavattisihanada Sutta; *The Long Discourses of the Buddha:* 395–405
18. *Anguttara Nikaya V:* Sona Vagga: Sona Sutta

19. *Anguttara Nikaya V:* Upasaka Vagga: Gihi Sutta

20. *Samyutta Nikaya V:* Sotapatti Samyutta: Veludvareyya Sutta; *The Connected Discourses of the Buddha:* 1796–1799

21. *Digha Nikaya I:* 8; *The Long Discourses of the Buddha:* 151–157

22. *Anguttara Nikaya V:* Aghata Vagga: Codana Sutta

23. *Digha Nikaya III:* 31: Sigalovada Sutta; *The Long Discourses of the Buddha:* 461–469

24. Ibid.

25. *Sutta Nipata:* Culla Vagga: Mangala Sutta

26. *Anguttara Nikaya IV:* Kesi Vagga: Kesi Sutta

27. *Digha Nikaya III:* 31: Sigalovada Sutta; *The Long Discourses of the Buddha:* 461–469

28. *Majjhima Nikaya III:* 101: Devadaha Sutta; *The Middle Length Discourses of the Buddha:* 827–838

29. *Majjhima Nikaya III:* 112: Chabbisodana Sutta; *The Middle Length Discourses of the Buddha:* 903–908

30. *Majjhima Nikaya III:* 101: Devadaha Sutta; *The Middle Length Discourses of the Buddha:* 827–838

31. *Samyutta Nikaya V:* Sotapatti Samyutta: Veludvareyya Sutta; *The Connected Discourses of the Buddha:* 1796–1799

32. *Majjhima Nikaya III:* 101: Devadaha Sutta; *The Middle Length Discourses of the Buddha:* 827–838

33. Ibid.

CHAPTER 13

Epigraph taken from: *Anguttara Nikaya III:* Bala Vagga: Lakkhana Sutta

1. *Digha Nikaya I:* 4: Sonadanda Sutta; *The Long Discourses of the Buddha:* 125–132

2. *Sutta Nipata:* Uraga Vagga: Vasala Sutta

3. *Anguttara Nikaya VI:* Maha Vagga: Nibbedhika Sutta

4. *Majjhima Nikaya II:* 61: Ambalatthikarahulovada Sutta; *The Middle Length Discourses of the Buddha:* 523–526

5. *Dhammapada:* Verse 252

6. *Anguttara Nikaya III:* Bala Vagga: Accaya Sutta

7. *Anguttara Nikaya III:* Puggala Vagga: Jigucchitabba Sutta

8. *Majjhima Nikaya I:* 15: Anumana Sutta; *The Middle Length Discourses of the Buddha:* 190–193

9. Ibid.

10. *Majjhima Nikaya I:* 10: Satipatthana Sutta; *The Middle Length Discourses of the Buddha:* 145–155

11. *Majjhima Nikaya I:* 15: Anumana Sutta; *The Middle Length Discourses of the Buddha:* 190–193

12. *Majjhima Nikaya II:* 58: Abhayarajakumara Sutta; *The Middle Length Discourses of the Buddha:* 498–501

13. *Majjhima Nikaya II:* 61: Ambalatthikarahulovada Sutta; *The Middle Length Discourses of the Buddha:* 523–526

14. *Anguttara Nikaya VI:* Sacitta Vagga: Sariputta Sutta

15. *Majjhima Nikaya I:* 15: Anumana Sutta; *The Middle Length Discourses of the Buddha:* 190–193

16. *Anguttara Nikaya III:* Sambodhi Vagga: Arakkhita Sutta

17. *Anguttara Nikaya III:* Bala Vagga: Cinta Sutta

18. *Dhammapada:* Verses 3–4

CHAPTER 14

Epigraph taken from: *Dhammapada:* Verses 199 and 204

1. *Anguttara Nikaya I:* Pamada Vagga: 9

2. *Anguttara Nikaya III:* Devaduta Vagga, Hatthaka Sutta

   Note: The Pali sentence is *yeca pana loke sukham senti so tesu aham accayo.* Literally, *sukham senti* is "sleep happily," but its actual meaning is "live happily."

3. *Vinaya Pitaka:* Maha Vagga: 1. 11

4. Internet Edition of CNN news (Health), May 22, 2003

5. Internet Edition of BBC news, May 21, 2003

6. Ibid.

7. *Dhammapada:* Verse 165

8. *Dhammapada:* Verse 276

9. *Anguttara Nikaya III:* Maha Vagga: Titthayatana Sutta

10. *Proceedings of the National Academy of Sciences,* November 16, 2004

11. *Discoverychannel.com:* "Study: Meditation Changes Monks' Outlook," Anna Salleh, June 7, 2005

12. *Majjhima Nikaya II:* 79: Culasakuludayi Sutta; *The Middle Length Discourses of the Buddha:* 654–662

13. *Majjhima Nikaya III:* 86: Angulimala Sutta; *The Middle Length Discourses of the Buddha:* 710–717

14. *Samyutta Nikaya I:* Devata Samyutta: Aranna Sutta; *The Connected Discourses of the Buddha:* 93

15. *Majjhima Nikaya III:* 132: Anandabhaddekaratta Sutta; *The Middle Length Discourses of the Buddha:* 523–526
16. *Dhammapada:* Verse 157
17. *Majjhima Nikaya I:* 18: Madhupindika Sutta; *The Middle Length Discourses of the Buddha:* 201–206
18. Ibid.
19. *Dhammapada:* Verse 216
20. *Dhammapada:* Verse 197
21. *Anguttara Nikaya I:* Pabhassara Vagga: Pabhassara Sutta
22. *Majjhima Nikaya III:* 118: Anapanasati Sutta; *The Middle Length Discourses of the Buddha:* 941–948
23. Ibid.
24. *Digha Nikaya III:* 29: Pasadika Sutta; *The Middle Length Discourses of the Buddha:* 427–439
25. *Dhammapada:* Verse 198
26. *Dhammapada:* Verse 183
27. *Anguttara Nikaya IV:* Pattakamma Vagga: Anana Sutta
28. *Dhammapada:* Verse 69
29. *Samyutta Nikaya I:* Kosala Samyutta: Donapaka Sutta; *The Connected Discourses of the Buddha:* 176–177
30. *Dhammapada:* Verse 277
31. Ibid.
32. *Vinaya Pitaka:* Maha Vagga:1. 11

ACKNOWLEDGMENTS

Several renowned personalities have written about this books. Most prominent among them is communication satellite pioneer and science fiction guru Sir Arthur C. Clarke. I am honored to have the foreword from this legendary writer whose books have mesmerized and enlightened the entire world.

Ven. Henepola Gunaratana Thero, a writer on Buddha's teachings and a prominent meditation teacher in America, and Anne C. Klein, professor of Buddhist studies at Rice University in Houston, Texas, wrote reviews on this book. I thank them sincerely for showing their appreciation of this work.

Finally, I would like to express my thanks to Wisdom Publications and especially to its senior editor Josh Bartok for showing appreciation of this book and deciding to publish it.

Bhikkhu Basnagoda Rahula
Vipassana Meditation Retreat
Willis, Texas
January 20, 2008

Born in Sri Lanka, Bhikkhu Basnagoda Rahula became, during his childhood, a novice monk at Attanagalla Royal Temple in his native country. After receiving High Ordination and a bachelor's degree in Buddhist philosophy, he emigrated to the United States in 1990.

Bhikkhu Rahula earned his M.A. in literature from the University of Houston–Clear Lake and his Ph.D. in English from Texas Tech University in Lubbock, Texas. Currently, he serves the congregation of Vipassana Meditation Retreat in Willis, Texas, as its president while teaching English at the University of Houston–Downtown.

ABOUT WISDOM PUBLICATIONS

Wisdom Publications, a nonprofit publisher, is dedicated to making available authentic works relating to Buddhism for the benefit of all. We publish books by ancient and modern masters in all traditions of Buddhism, translations of important texts, and original scholarship. Additionally, we offer books that explore East-West themes unfolding as traditional Buddhism encounters our modern culture in all its aspects. Our titles are published with the appreciation of Buddhism as a living philosophy, and with the special commitment to preserve and transmit important works from Buddhism's many traditions.

To learn more about Wisdom, or to browse books online, visit our website at www.wisdompubs.org.

You may request a copy of our catalog online or by writing to this address:

Wisdom Publications
199 Elm Street
Somerville, Massachusetts 02144 USA
Telephone: 617-776-7416
Fax: 617-776-7841
Email: info@wisdompubs.org
www.wisdompubs.org

THE WISDOM TRUST

As a nonprofit publisher, Wisdom is dedicated to the publication of Dharma books for the benefit of all sentient beings and dependent upon the kindness and generosity of sponsors in order to do so. If you would like to make a donation to Wisdom, you may do so through our website or our Somerville office. If you would like to help sponsor the publication of a book, please write or email us at the address above.

Thank you.

Wisdom is a nonprofit, charitable 501(c)(3) organization affiliated with the Foundation for the Preservation of the Mahayana Tradition (FPMT).

ALSO AVAILABLE FROM WISDOM PUBLICATIONS

In the Buddha's Words
An Anthology of Discourses from the Pali Canon
Edited and introduced by Bhikkhu Bodhi
Foreword by the Dalai Lama
512 pp, ISBN 0-86171-491-1, $18.95

This landmark collection is the definitive introduction to the Buddha's teachings—in his own words. The American scholar-monk Bhikkhu Bodhi, whose voluminous translations have won widespread acclaim, here presents selected discourses of the Buddha from the Pali Canon, the earliest record of what the Buddha taught. Divided into ten thematic chapters, *In the Buddha's Words* reveals the full scope of the Buddha's discourses, from family life and marriage to renunciation and the path of insight. A concise, informative introduction precedes each chapter, guiding the reader toward a deeper understanding of the texts that follow.

In the Buddha's Words allows even readers unacquainted with Buddhism to grasp the significance of the Buddha's contributions to our world heritage. Taken as a whole, these texts bear eloquent testimony to the breadth and intelligence of the Buddha's teachings, and point the way to an ancient yet ever-vital path. Students and seekers alike will find this systematic presentation indispensable.

"Any amount of study or practice that helps to deepen wisdom and assist us to emerge from layers of delusion is precious. This book could contribute to this enterprise more than almost anything else in print."—Andrew Olendzki, Executive Director of the Barre Center of Buddhist Studies, in *Buddhadharma: The Practitioner's Quarterly*

Mindfulness in Plain English
Revised, Expanded Edition
Bhante Gunaratana
224 pages, ISBN 0-86171-321-4, $14.95

"Extremely up-to-date and approachable, this book also serves as a very thorough FAQ for new (and not-so-new) meditators. Bhante has an engaging delivery and a straightforward voice that's hard not to like."—*Shambhala Sun*

"Of great value to newcomers, especially those without access to a teacher."—Larry Rosenberg, author of *Breath by Breath*

The Four Foundations of Mindfulness
Venerable U Silananda
256 pages, ISBN 0-86171-328-1, $16.95

"The Maha Satipatthana Sutta, the Great Discourse on the Foundations of Mindfulness, is one of the key teachings of the Buddha, and Venerable U Silananda has written one of its best and most illuminating commentaries."—Sharon Salzberg, author of *Lovingkindness*

"*The Four Foundations of Mindfulness* is, like all of Wisdom's books, beautiful in all respects."— Jon Kabat-Zinn, author of *Wherever You Go, There You Are*